# GENEALOGICAL TROVES

Also by Dennis Ford

Fiction
~ *Red Star*
~ *Landsman*
~ *Things Don't Add Up*
~ *The Watchman*

Humor / Belles Lettres
~ *Thinking About Everything*
~ *Miles of Thoughts*

Family History
~ *Eight Generations*
~ *Genealogical Jaunts*
~ *Genealogical Musings*

Psychology
~ *Lectures on Theories of Learning*
~ *Lectures on General Psychology ~ Volume One*
~ *Lectures on General Psychology ~ Volume Two*

# GENEALOGICAL TROVES

## VOLUME ONE

DENNIS FORD

# GENEALOGICAL TROVES
## VOLUME ONE

*iUniverse books may be ordered through booksellers or by contacting:*

*iUniverse*
*1663 Liberty Drive*
*Bloomington, IN 47403*
*www.iuniverse.com*
*1-800-Authors (1-800-288-4677)*

*The cover photograph is of the "Virgin Rock" in the Atlantic at Ballybunion.*

*ISBN: 978-1-5320-8668-7 (sc)*
*ISBN: 978-1-5320-8669-4 (e)*

*Library of Congress Control Number: 2019917148*

*Print information available on the last page.*

*iUniverse rev. date: 10/24/2019*

To the people of the past, that we remember them

# Contents

# Preface

On and off for the past quarter century I've collected Irish genealogical records. Initially, these records pertained to my ancestors and their ancestral townlands. Records were copied off microfilm readers at the Mormon Family History Library at 65th St. and Columbus Ave. in Manhattan. Records were also ordered from the Registrar's Office in Ireland and from Heritage Centers in Counties Mayo, Roscommon and Kerry. A recent bloom of on-line resources allowed for a massive expansion of record collection. Using these on-line resources, I decided to collect as many records as possible pertaining to my surnames. These records were copied while seated at my kitchen table in front of my laptop. Unlike in previous years, almost everything can be collected without leaving the comforts of home.

The present volume, which is expected to be the first of two, includes the following predominantly 19th century records pertaining to:

- Forde families residing in the vicinity of Ballyhaunis in County Mayo.
- Freeman families residing in the vicinity of Ballyhaunis in County Mayo.
- Allen families residing in the vicinity of Ballybunion in County Kerry.
- Linnane families residing in the vicinity of Ballybunion in County Kerry.

~ families in the townland of Laughil in Kiltullagh Parish, County Roscommon.

~ families in the townland of Derrynacong in Annagh Parish, County Mayo.

Roman Catholic parish registers are available on-line at *www.registers.nli.ie*. The records terminate circa 1880. (Microfilm records at the Family History Library continued into the 20th century.) The records are searchable by event and date, not by name. The legibility of the records, which are in PDF format, varies greatly.

Civil records of births, deaths and marriages are available at *www.irishgenealogy.ie*. The records extend roughly from 1864 into the 1950s. They are searchable by name, date and civil registration district. (The latter facilitates searches, but is not required.) In addition, the website contains select Roman Catholic records searchable by name, year and parish. Luckily for my surnames, the records for North Kerry parishes are available on the website.

Census records for 1901 and 1911 are available at *www.census.nationalarchives.ie*. The records are searchable by name and townland. PDF images of the census forms are available to download and print.

Land records are available on-line at the Valuation Office at *www.irish-geneaography.com/valuation-office*. The records are searchable by surname and parish. For North Kerry, these records slightly predate Griffith's Valuation. Records are scarce for the Mayo and Roscommon vicinities recorded in *Troves*. There are a number of websites pertaining to the Tithe Applotment books and to Griffith's Valuation.

The website *Findmypast* has collected a huge trove of 19th century records, most valuably records of the local petty courts. (Incredibly, records of dog licenses are available.) The records, which are available for a modest monthly fee, are searchable by name and townland.

All records in *Genealogical Troves ~ Volume One* need to be verified. There may be errors in transcription—informants may have provided inaccurate details; priests and civil registrars may have erred in recording events; researchers who digitized the records may have made errors; shamefully, I may have erred in copying names and dates.

Older parish records, especially in Annagh Parish, Mayo, are often illegible in places. Reading them is a projective test of interpretation. In addition, dates in the older registers are frequently jumbled. Pages in the parish books are not always in chronological order. I elected to include only the month and year of individual records, but both months and years need to be verified by users of this book. In some cases I was able to include only the year.

Dates of births and deaths in civil records should be considered approximations of the actual events. Since families had several months to report events, it often happens that dates in civil records do not correspond with dates in the church registers. Irish babies are frequently found to be baptized before they are reported as born, a situation no less amazing than the Mormon practice of baptizing deceased people. In addition, ages in civil death records should be considered approximations of the actual ages. Frequently, informants had only a rough idea of the decedents' actual ages.

Family records in *Genealogical Troves* should be considered incomplete— this is especially the case with the older records. The records of baptisms and marriages of persons born before the commencement of church registers are permanently lost. Deaths and burials were not recorded by the churches included in this book. Illegibility of parish records may have resulted in missed or in faulty interpretations of names and dates. Pages may be missing from the extant registers. Families may not have reported events to the civil authorities. Errors of transcription may have occurred.

For the reasons listed above, townland records in *Genealogical Troves* should also be considered incomplete. Census records can be used to supplement church and civil records.

Family records are in chronological order from the first occurrence of surnames in parish books and civil records. Similarly, records for Laughil and Derrynacong are in chronological order from the first occurrence of surnames. The names of godparents and witnesses are in parentheses. Throughout, I've used a question mark (?) to indicate uncertainties in copying names and dates.

# Sources

*Forde Families in the Vicinity of Ballyhaunis*

Bekan Parish books, 1832 – 1920
Kiltullagh Parish books, 1839 - 1880
Annagh Parish books, 1851 - 1920
Tuam Archdiocese Marriage books, 1820s
Civil Records, 1865 – 1920 (marriages & deaths)


*Freeman Families in the Vicinity of Ballyhaunis*

Bekan Parish books, 1832 – 1920
Kiltullagh Parish books, 1846 - 1880
Annagh Parish books, 1851 – 1920
Aghamore Parish books, 1864 – 1920
Tuam Archdiocese Marriage books, 1820s
Civil Records, 1865 – 1926 (marriages), 1865 - 1964 (deaths)

*Allen Families in the Vicinity of Ballybunion*

Ballybunion and Ballylongford Parish books, 1832 – 1920
Listowel Parish books, 1808 – 1920
Tarbert Parish books, 1796 – 1914
Valuation Office House & Tenure books, 1850
Civil Records, 1868 – 1952 (marriages & deaths)


*Linnane Families in the Vicinity of Ballybunion*

Ballybunion and Ballylongford Parish books, 1832 – 1920
Listowel Parish books, 1808 – 1920
Valuation Office House & Tenure books, 1848 - 1852
Civil Records, 1864 – 1909 (marriages), 1879 – 1920 (deaths)


*Laughil Townland, Kiltullagh Parish, County Roscommon*

Kiltullagh Parish books, 1839 – 1880
Civil Records, 1864 – 1911 (marriages), 1871 – 1934 (deaths)
Findmypast - Petty Court Records (1853 – 1901)


*Derrynacong Townland, Annagh Parish, County Mayo*

Annagh Parish books, 1851 – 1920
Civil Records, 1864 – 1931 (marriages), 1868 – 1959 (deaths)
Findmypast - Petty Court Records (1856 – 1912)

# Forde Families in the Vicinity of Ballyhaunis, County Mayo, in the 19th Century

There are four origins of the surname Forde in Ireland. The likeliest origin for the Forde surname in the vicinity of Ballyhaunis derives from the Irish *Mac Giolla na Naomh*, which translates as "son of the servant of the saint." This sept name, in turn, was rendered as *Mac Giollarnath*, which translates as "son of the servant of the ford."

A second Connacht sept derives from the Irish *Mac Consnamha*, which translates "son of the expert swimmer." This sept is believed to be less common in the vicinity of Ballyhaunis.

The third origin of the Forde surname derives from *O Fuarrain*, which translates as "descendent of the cold one." This sept is located in County Cork. Finally, there were English named Forde who settled in Counties Meath and Louth during the Norman invasion and later.

The name is spelled inconsistently in civil and parish records as "Forde" and as "Ford." Spelling has been standardized as "Forde."

The use of the term "Bekan" indicates the parish and not the townland of that name, unless specified.

## Viscount Dillon Book of Leases

Charles Forde, Carrowmore, Knock, 1800

## Diocese of Tuam Marriage Records

Margaret Forde & Andrew Higgins
m. May 1823 (Richard Morelly & Marcella B-?), Bekan Parish

Bridget Forde & John Kenny
m. Feb. 1824 (John Forde & Michael Mulkeen), Bekan

Sally Forde & Tobias Kilkenny
m. Feb. 1824 (Thomas Kilkenny & Michael Kilkenny), Bekan

Peggy Forde & Michael Grealy (Greaty)
m. June 1825 (John & Mary Forde), Bekan

Mary Forde & John Joyce
m. Jan. 1826 (John Forde & Nicholas Joyce), Annagh Parish

John Forde & Mary Killeen
m. Feb. 1826 (John Killeen & Michael Forde), Annagh

John Forde & Sally Waldron
m. Apr. 1826 (Thomas & Mary Waldron), Bekan

Michael Forde & Honor Leech
m. March 1827 (Pat Leech & Mary Kean), Aghamore & Knock Parish

John Forde & Mary Falmon
m. May 1827 (Pat Falman & Augustin Falman), Annagh

Tithe Applotment Books - January 1835

Widow Forde & Co., Hazelhill, Annagh

Michael Forde & Co., Grallagh or Johnstown, Annagh

Patrick Forde, Carrownamonis?, Annagh

Daniel Forde & Co., Larganboy, Bekan

Charles Forde, Carramore, Knock Parish


Griffith's Valuation - 1856

Patrick Forde, Abbeyquarter, Annagh Parish

John Forde, Cloontumper

Patrick Forde, Derrynacong

Andrew Forde, Grallagh

Honoria Forde, Bracklaghboy, Bekan Parish

Francis Forde, Erriff

Francis Forde, Greenwood

John Forde, Island

Thomas Forde, Island

Thomas Forde, Island

John Forde, Larganboy East
Mary Forde

James Forde, Larganboy East

*Dennis Ford*

Honoria Forde

Patrick Forde, Larganboy East

James Forde, Larganboy West
Patrick Forde
Mary Forde
Michael Forde

Michael Forde, Larganboy West

Patrick Forde, Larganboy West
Mary Forde
James Forde

Michael Forde (Michael), Reask
Michael Forde (Bawn)
Michael Forde (Hugh)
Anthony Forde

Francis Forde, Turlough

Mary Forde, Ballinross, <u>Kiltullagh Parish</u>

William Forde, Laughil

Charles Forde, Churchfield, <u>Knock Parish</u>

John Forde, Eskerymorilly

Patrick Forde, Srah

Note: Patrick Forde of Abbeyquarter was a licensed publican. There's an Apr. 1842 record for Patrick Forde of Abbeyquarter in the House Books kept by the Valuation Office.

<u>Annagh, Bekan & Kiltullagh Parish Registers, Baptisms & Marriages</u>

John Forde & Sabina Waldron
m. Apr. 1826 (Thomas & Mary Waldron), Bekan [see Tuam marriage record]
Mary, Apr. 1833 (Anddrew Hopkins & Honor Delaney)
John, July 1835 (Frank Forde & Mary Ward)
Bridget, 1836 (Honor? & Michael Hopkins)
Anne, 1839 (Thomas Forde & Bridget Hopkins) [record requires verification]
Bridget, 1840 (John Mulclean & Catherine Walsh)

Thomas Forde & Mary Ward
Mary, Jan. 1833 (Pat Forde & Honor Swift), Bekan
Bridget, Dec. 1834 (John & Margaret Forde)
Catherine, 1837 (John Forde & Mary Ward)
Ellen, Augt. 1838 (John & Margaret Forde)
Thomas, 1844 (Dominick Neiland &? Walsh)

Mary Forde & Austin Grogan
Julia, March 1833 (Denis Grogan & Catherine Comber), Bekan
Bridget, 1836 (L. Grogan & Bridget Forde)
Thomas, 1840 (? Finn &?)

Michael Forde & Mary Forde
m. Jan. 1834 (Catherine Connelly), Bekan
Sarah, 1838 (Bartly Mulclean? & Anne Grogan)
Michael, Dec. 1852 (Michael Forde & Sara Forde),

Patrick Forde & Catherine Finn
m. Feb. 1834 (Thomas Forde & Mary Forde), Bekan [record requires verification]
John, 1836 (John Forde & Sarah Grogan)
Patrick, 1839 (Bridget Forde & L.Voy?) [record requires verification]
Catherine, Augt. 1845 (James & Catherine Forde)

Mary? Forde & Eugene Nolan
Penelope, Oct. 1834 (John Forde & Cathy Nolan), Bekan

Thomas Forde & Mary Grogan

Mary, Dec. 1834 (David Lyons & Mary Daly), Bekan

Mary Forde & Michael Folliard, Bekan
m. May 1835 (John Fitzgerald & Margaret?)

Note: Michael's surname requires verification – it may be "Filand" or "Niland."

Honor Forde & Martin Judge
m. July 1835 (Pat & Sarah Mullin), Bekan
Mary, 1836 (Bartl. Mulclean & Nelly Forde)
Francis & Sarah 1841 (John &? Forde) [record requires verification]
Catherine, Feb. 1847 (Catherine?)
Martin, Sept. 1852 (Michael Forde & Anne Forde)
Mary, July, 1854 (William Kirrane & Mary Forde)
Mary, July 1857 (Michael Kirrane & Mary Forde)

Note: for baptism of Mary, 1836, parish register notes "not charged, paupers."

Austin Forde & Mary Larky?
Julia, Sept. 1835 (D. & Mary Waldron or Killian), Bekan
child, June 1847 (John Forde &?) [record requires verification]

Daniel Forde & Honora Mulhearn
Bridget, Dec. 1835 (J. Hopkins &? Forde), Bekan

?? Forde & Thomas MacKenna, Larganboy
Margaret, 1835 (Pat Grogan & Bridget Mulclean)

John Forde & Peggy Boyle
Mary, 1835, Bekan [record requires verification]

Thady Forde & Catherine Kieran (Kirrane)
m. Feb. 1836 (Thomas Kieran & Mary Dyer), Bekan

Michael Forde & Mary Lyons
m. March 1836 (Pat McGarry & Bridget Lyons), Bekan

James Forde & Catherine Hopkins

James, Nov. 1836 (Thomas Forde & Mary Mulclear), Bekan
James, 1838 (Peter Hopkins &? Forde)
Mary, 1842 (James Waldron & Mary Hopkins)
Richard, Augt. 1845 (Michael Hopkins & Mary Hopkins)

Michael Forde & Mary Grogan
Pat, 1836 (Pat &? Grogan), Bekan
Bridget, Apr. 1845 (Thomas Hunt & Mary Mulqueen)
Mary, March 1848 (John Bentson? & Honora Hunt?)
Thomas, Dec. 1849 (Thomas & Honora Forde)
child, Apr. 1851 (? Grogan)
Anne, Nov. 1852 (Thomas Waldron & Bridget Hunt)
Ellen, Augt. 1855 (Denis Grogan & Mary Fitzmaurice)

Michael Forde & Honoria Swift
Catherine, 1836 (Thomas Grealy & Margaret McGreal?), Bekan
Michael, 1838 (James Grealy & Margaret Groak)

Bridget Forde & Enias? Killeen
m. Apr. 1837 (Michael & Bridget Killeen), Bekan

James Forde & Ellen Finn
m. Jan. 1838 (Darby Finn & Catherine McHale), Derra, Bekan
Anne, 1842 (Pat Waldron & Mary Mulkean)
Bridget, Sept. 1848 (Darby Finn & Catherine Healy)
Ellen, Dec. 1853 (Michael & Mary Forde)

Anne Forde & James Harkin
Patrick, Nov. 1838 (Anthony Grogan & Bridget Freeman), Clooncrim, Kiltullagh Parish
James, July 1841 (Mary Flatley)
Bridget, Dec. 1842 (Pat Harkin & Bridget Forde)
child, 1845 (Winifred Forde)

John Forde & Catherine Forde
Mary, Apr. 1839 (Pat & Mary Forde), Bekan

Pat Forde & Bridget Reynolds

Honor & Judith, Sept. 1840 (S. Burke & M. Daly), Levallyroe, Kiltullagh

Note: it's not certain the above are twins or one child with two personal names.

Pat Forde & Mary Flanagan
Thady, Oct. 1840 (Pat Kenny & Mary Burke), Mount Devlin, Kiltullagh
Honor, Apr. 1847 (Mary Kenny?)

James Forde & Catherine Finn
Mary, 1840 (Michael Forde & Peggy Finn), Bekan
Catherine, Nov. 1845 (Pat Finn & Mary Forde)

Note: this may be the same family listed above as James Forde & Ellen Finn.

Ellen Forde & Owen Nowlan
Bridget, 1840 (Thomas Mulclear & Bridget Nowlan), Bekan

Pat Forde & Eleanor Fahy
m. Feb. 1841 (Michael Tierney & Bridget Forde), Clogher, Kiltullagh
Bridget, Dec. 1841 (Mary Sweeney)
Mary, July 1844 (Bryan Green & Bridget Forde)

Michael Forde & Catherine?
Bridget & Susan, July 1841 (Martin Judge & Pat Judge; Catherine Grogan &?) Larganboy

Michael Forde & Kate Cruise
Bridget, Dec. 1841 (? Forde & Mary Cruise), Reask
Mary, Augt. 1845 (James Cruise & Bridget Groake)
Bridget, Feb. 1847 (Michael Connally &? Forde)
Catherine, Nov. 1849 (Pat Jordan? & Bridget Groake)

Catherine Forde & Thomas Blyghe?
m. Feb. 1842 (Peter Kenny & Bridget Forde), Clogher, Kiltullagh

Francis Forde & Catherine Egan
Pat, 1842 (Thomas Comber & Mary Higgins), Bekan
Mary, 1844 (James Egan &? Forde)

Bridget, Dec. 1852 (Patrick Forde & Mary Egan)
Margaret, Jan. 1855 (Patrick Comber & Bridget Egan)
Catherine, Sept. 1857 (Thomas Calkeen? & Catherine Egan)

Mary Forde & James Dyer
m. July 1843 (Michael & Margaret Grealy), Reask
Bridget. Feb. 1847 (John Forde & Mary Dyer) [record requires verification]
John, March 1848 (Michael Forde &? Noone)

Sara Forde & Peter Commons
James, Oct. 1843 (Bryan Delaney & Bridget Rogers), Lowberry, Kiltullagh
Thomas, Dec. 1845 (Bessy Forde)
Mary, Nov. 1848 (Margaret Byrne)

Rose Forde & James Hopkins
m. Feb. 1845 (James Hopkins & Mary?), Bekan
Pat, Feb. 1849 (James Forde & Catherine Hopkins)
Daniel, Oct. 1853 (John Forde & Judith Hopkins)
Mary, July, 1854 (Pat Hopkins & Bridget Forde)
Peter, Dec. 1855 (Michael Hopkins & Sabina Flynn)

John Forde & Mary Murphy
Patrick, Feb. 1845 (Michael Forde & Bridget Murphy), Bekan
Michael, Jan. 1847 (Michael & Judy Forde)
John, Augt. 1850 (Hugh Forde & Bridget Murphy)
Thomas, Dec. 1854 (Thomas Forde & Margaret Murphy)
Mary, Dec. 1857 (P. Murphy & Bridget Murphy)
Catherine, Feb. 1862 (James Forde & Bridget Larkin)

Bridget Forde & James Gilfoyle
m. Feb. 1845 (John Forde & Mary Carty), Levallyroe, Kiltullagh

William Forde & Mary Forde, Cloonberin?, Kiltullagh
m. Oct. 1845 (William Coley & Dan Forde)
Michael, Sept. 1846 (sponsors illegible)

Note: William was from Cloonberin. Mary was from Mount Devlin.

Francis Forde & Mary Egan
John, 1845, Bekan [record requires verification]
Margaret, Sept. 1846 (James Egan & Mary Egan)

Note: this may be the same family listed above as Francis Forde & Catherine Egan

Mary Forde & James?
Mary, July 1846 (Pat Forde &?), Bekan

Bridget Forde & James Quinn
Michael, 1846 (Michael &? Quinn), Bekan

Catherine Forde & Pat Nowland (Nolan?)
Bridget, March 1847 (J. Dyer & Mary Forde), Bekan

? Forde & John Prendergast
Catherine, Oct. 1847 (Michael & Kate Forde), Bekan

Bridget Forde & John Kilkenny
m. Oct. 1847 (Thomas Kilkenny & Kate Forde), Bekan
Kate, Augt. 1848 (John & Kate Forde)
Anthony, Nov. 1851 (Thomas Forde & Anne Fitzmaurice)
Mary, Dec. 1855 (Andrew & Catherine Forde)
Thomas, Dec. 1857 (Thomas? & Bridget Nolan)
James, Jan. 1862 (Andrew Forde & Mary Nolan)

Anne Forde & Patrick Mulkeen
m. March 1848 (Pat Ford & Mary Ford), Larganboy
Ellen, Augt. 1856 (Patrick Forde & Bridget Kilkenny)

Celia Forde & Edward Rush
Celia, Apr. 1850 (Mary Rush), Kiltullagh Parish

Andrew Forde & Kate Kelly
Honoria, Nov. 1851 (Mary Hunt), Churchpark, Annagh
Andrew, Nov. 1853 (John Kelly & Mary Lyons)

Bridget Forde & John Higgins

Honoria, Apr. 1852 (Edward Morley & Bridget Connally), Bekan

Michael Forde & Bridget Fitzmaurice
Mary, Augt. 1852 (Pat & Anne Fitzmaurice), Reask
Thomas, Dec. 1854 (Michael Forde & Bridget Morley)
Judith, Feb. 1860 (Anthony Forde & Bridget Fitzmaurice)
Bridget, Dec. 1862 (Thomas Forde & Catherine Forde)
John, June, 1864 (civil record)
Anne, Sept. 1867 (Michael Forde & Mary Fitzmaurice)
Andrew, Oct. 1869 (Thomas Forde & Mary Fitzmaurice)
Ellen, Sept. 1872 (Peter Fitzmaurice & Mary Lydon?; Anne Veasy, present)

Pat Forde & Jane Agnes O'Neil
m. Dec. 1852 (Roger Judge & Kate Diskin), Kiltullagh Parish

Patrick Forde & Catherine Grogan
m. Jan. 1853 (James Forde & Mary Forde), Larganboy
Daniel, Dec. 1853 (James & Rose Forde)
Mary, July 1854 (Denis McGrath & Bridget Grogan)
Honoria, Oct. 1855 (John Grogan & Mary Nolan)
Mary, July 1857 (Denis McGraf & Bridget Grogan)
Catherine, Nov. 1862 (John Forde & Rose Forde)
Patrick, 1864 (Patrick Hopkins & Mary Mulhearn)
John, Oct. 1866 (Margaret Mulkeen present)
Bridget, Augt. 1868 (civil record, Honoria Forde present)

Thomas Forde & Bridget Waldron
m. March 1853 (Pat Grogan & Bridget Waldron), Reask
Michael, Dec. 1853 (Martin Waldron & Rose Caulfield)
Patrick, Jan. 1855 (Hugh Forde & Cecilia Fitzgerald)
John, Oct. 1856 (Michael Waldron & Honora Fitzmaurice)
Martin, June, 1857 (Michael Forde & Bridget Flynn)
Martin, June 1858 (Anthony Forde & Bridget Waldron)
Martin, June 1860 (Michael Forde & Bridget Forde)
Thomas, June 1862 (Michael Waldron)
Mary, Dec. 1863 (Michael Forde & Catherine Fitzmaurice)
Catherine & Bridget, May 1866 (civil record)
Julia, Sept. 1867 (Michael Forde & T. Prendergast)

Andrew, Feb. 1869 (? & Mary Forde)

Patrick Forde & Bridget Freeman
Michael, June 1853 (John Freely? & Catherine Dyer), Derrynacong, Annagh
Thomas, July 1856 (Henry & Anne Hamrock)
Hubert, June 1858 (Mary Hunt)

Mary Forde & Edward Comber
m. Jan. 1854 (John Grogan & Mary Mulkeen), Greenwood
Bridget, June 1854 (Cormack Flynn & Bridget Comber)
James, Nov.1865 (civil record; Catherine Forde present)

Patrick Forde & Anne Finn
m. Feb. 1854 (Thomas & Mary Forde), Larganboy
Mary, Sept. 1857 (Michael Finn & Bridget Finn)
Patrick, Jan. 1862 (Edward Finn & Bridget Forde)
Bridget, Augt. 1863 (M. Finn & Honoria Flynn)
Anne & Julia, Jan. 1866 (Pat Finn & Cath. Forde; James & Bridget Forde)
Michael, July 1867 (James & Bridget Forde)
Hugh, July 1869 (Judith Hopkins)

Mary Forde & Patrick Judge
m. Feb. 1854 (James Grealy & Margaret Forde), Ballindrehid, Bekan
Catherine, Dec. 1856 (Andrew Forde & Mary Swift)
Bridget, Dec. 1863 (Thomas Moran & Anne Forde)
Mary, May 1867 (civil record)
child, June 1869 (civil record; child died 1869)
Anne, Augt. 1870 (civil record)
Patrick, Dec. 1871 (Michael Lyons & Mary Lyons)
Thomas, Nov. 1874 (James Cunnane & Mary Henry)

John Forde & Mary Groake
Mary, Dec. 1854 (Bridget Brown & Owen Harken), Kiltullagh Parish
William, Oct. 1858 (John Harkin & Honoria Flynn)

Catherine Forde & James Kilkenny
m. Feb. 1855 (John & Catherine Kilkenny), Bekan

Winifred Forde & Thomas Fahy
m. Dec. 1855 (Thomas Fleming & Kate M?), Kiltullagh Parish
Thady, July 1857 (Martin Quinn & Margaret Fleming)

William Forde & Margaret Hoban
m. Dec. 1856 (Patrick Johnson & Mary Reily, in Bekan Parish), Laughil,
Kiltullagh
Mary, Sept. 1857 (Pat Hoban & Kate Forde)
Thomas, Jan. 1860 (Thomas Hoban & Margaret Hoban)
Catherine, Nov. 1862 (Thomas Hoban & Bridget Fitzmaurice)
"churched Mrs. William Forde," Nov. 1866
Bridget, Sept. 1869 (Pat Forde & Catherine Frehily)
William, Sept. 1872 (Peter Flynn & Mary Killian; Mary Forde present)

John Forde & Mary Flynn
m. Jan. 1857 (Pat Harkan & Anne Flynn), Kiltullagh Parish
Mary, Dec. 1857 (Pat Harkin & Ann Flynn)
Patrick, Feb. 1859 (Pat Flanagan & Ellen Forde)

Anthony Forde & Catherine Hopkins
m. Jan. 1857 (William Forde & Honor Ruane), Bekan

Michael Forde & Mary Flanagan
Bridget, Feb. 1857 (Thomas Walsh & Mary Forde), Kiltullagh Parish

Thomas Forde & Judith Grogan
m. Apr. 1857 (John Kilkenny & Mary Nowlan), Larganboy
Augustine, Augt. 1858 (Pat Nolan & Bridget Forde)
Thomas, Dec. 1860 (Laurence & Bridget Grogan)
Andrew, March 1865 (civil record)
Bridget, Sept. 1867 (Pat McDonough & Judy Hopkins?)
Catherine, Oct. 1869 (Daniel Forde & Catherine Dyer)
Mary, Dec. 1871 (Michael Kelly & Mary Grogan)
Anne, 1874 (Thomas Forde & Bridget Hopkins)

John Forde & Mary Raughteen
m. June 1858 (John Dowry & Kate Raughteen), Kiltullagh Parish

Thomas Forde & Mary Hunt
m. Feb. 1860 (Thomas Kelly? & Mary Hunt, in Annagh Parish), Reask
Catherine, Dec. 1861 (Patrick Hunt & Catherine Hunt
Patrick, Augt. 1864 (Hugh Forde & Catherine Hunt)
Anne, Dec. 1869 (Thomas Hunt? & Ellen Mulhearn)
Mary, Jan. 1873 (civil record)

Bridget Forde & John Fahy
m. Feb. 1861 (Pat Fahy & Bridget Forde), Larganboy
Mary, Augt. 1863 (Pat Forde & Rose Forde)
Patrick, Augt. 1865 (civil record; Mary Comber present)
James, Oct. 1867 (Pat Forde & Mary Forde)
Rose, March, 1871 (John & Honora Forde)
Honor Augt. 1875 (John & Mary Forde)

Anne Forde & Patrick Hopkins
m. Feb. 1861 (W. Waldron & Ellen Flynn), Larganboy
Bridget, June 1862 (Peter Hopkins &? Ford)
Michael, March 1874 (James Forde & Mary Forde)

John Forde & Judith Hopkins
m. March 1861 (John Forde & Penelope Hopkins), Larganboy
Honora, Jan. 1863 (David Hopkins & Bridget Forde)
Michael, Sept. 1864 (Augustine Hopkins & Catherine Grogan)
Daniel, Oct. 1866 (Pat & Bridget Hopkins)
Bridget, 1867 James & Margaret Harkin) [record requires verification]
Austin, 1869 (Daniel Forde & Mary Hopkins) [record requires verification]
James, Sept. 1871 (Peter Hopkins & Mary Brennan)
Patrick, Jan. 1874 (Dan Hopkins & Honor Forde)

William Forde & Honoria Hunt
m. March 1861 (Michael Waldron & Kitty Grogan), Reask
Michael, Nov. 1865 (Thomas & Catherine Forde)
Bridget, Oct. 1867 (Thomas Forde & Bridget Duggan)
Thomas, 1870 (Pat Forde & Catherine Moran) [record requires verification]
John, July 1875 (Pat & Mary Forde)

Margaret Forde & Dan Moran
Honor, May 1861 (Denis & Sarah Forde), Carrick, Kiltullagh Parish

Honor Forde & James Travers
m. Feb. 1862 (Michael Darcy & Bridget Forde), Cuilbeg, Bekan
Margaret, Nov. 1876 (Michael Killian & Catherine Killian)

Mary Forde & Patrick Lyons
Ellen, June 1862 (James Travers & Bridget Forde), Bekan

Bridget Forde & William Feeny
m. Feb. 1863 (Thomas Sullivan & Bridget Nolan), Carrow Beg, Annagh Parish
John, June 1864 (James Forde & Bridget Waldron)

Andrew Forde & Honor Caulfield
m. Jan. 1864 (John Kilkenny & Ellen McGarry)
John, Dec. 1865 (civil record), Bekan
Catherine, Oct. 1867 (Pat & Catherine Caulfield)
Bridget, Jan. 1870 (Pat Caulfield & Honor?)
Honor, May 1871 (Peter H. & Mary Healy)
Mary, Nov. 1872 (James Caulfield & Bridget McQuade)
Patrick, March 1876 (Pat Henican & Mary Henican)

Note: Andrew was the son of John Forde of Larganboy. Honor wasthe daughter of James Caulfield of Cloontumper.

John Forde & Mary Roughnane (Rockford)
Matthew, Feb. 1864 (civil record), Bohauns, Knock
Honoria, Oct. 1866 (civil record)
Anne, Oct. 1868 (civil record)

Thomas Forde & Margaret Keenan
Margaret Ellen, Apr. 1864 (civil record), Hazelhill
Anne, May 1867 (civil record)

Note: Thomas is described as a carpenter. His name also appears as Timothy.

Mary Forde & Michael Waldron
m. June 1864 (Michael Caulfield & Mary Hunt), Bekan

Note: Margaret was the daughter of Thomas Forde of Island. Michael was the son of Michael Waldron of Clagnagh.

John Forde & Mary Henry
Catherine, Jan. 1865 (Anthony Forde & Margaret Henry) Ballindrehid
Michael, July 1866 (Edward Lyons & Bridget Forde)
Mary, Dec. 1871 (Pat Forde & Mary McGuire)
Patrick, June 1874 (Andrew Forde & Catherine Judge)
Thomas, March 1876 (Thomas Greally & Bridget Henry)
Andrew, March 1878 (James Trealy? & Honoria Judge)
John Austin, 1880 (Pat Breheny & Bridget Greally)

Mary Forde & Patrick Deasy
Margaret, Augt. 1865 (James & Mary Kilgallon), Coogue, Aghamore
Anne, Sept. 1867 (civil record)
Anne, Nov. 1868 (James Burke & Bridget Carney)

Note: Patrick Deasy was described as a weaver.

William Forde & Margaret Kelly
Patrick, March 1866 (civil record), Kiltullagh Parish

Sara Forde & John Kenny
Thomas, Augt. 1866 (Michael Forde & Bridget Judge; Mary Forde present), Larganboy
Mary, Jan. 1868 (Michael & Bridget Forde)
Anne, Sept. 1870 (Thady Kenny & Anne Forde)
Michael & Catherine 1875 (Thady Kenny & Bt. Judge; Peter Doyle & Bt. Kenny)

Patrick Forde & Mary Anne Gordon
Bridget, Sept. 1866 (civil record), Kiltullagh Parish

William Forde & Margaret Culliney
m. Feb. 1867 (John Murray (Morley) & Mary Grogan), Coolnafarna, Annagh
Bridget, Jan. 1868 (civil record)

Mary Ann, Dec. 1869 (civil record)

Note: William was the son of Timothy Forde of Cloonfaghna. Margaret was the daughter of Michael Culliney of Treanrevagh?

Catherine Forde & Owen Nolan
m. Feb. 1867 (Pat Forde & Bridget Forde), Mountain, Bekan
John, Jan. 1868 (civil record)
Dominick, July 1869 (civil record)
Thomas, Augt.1878 (Dominick Nolan & Margaret Lyons)
Catherine, Nov.1880 (John & Ellen?)
Ellen, Sept. 1883 (John & Mary Greally)

Note: Catherine was the daughter of Michael Forde of Reask. Owen was the son of Owen Nolan of Mountain.

Bridget Forde & Patrick Caulfield
m. March 1867 (Matthew McGuire & Bridget Forde), Ballindrehid
Catherine, Dec. 1868 (civil record)
Patrick, Apr. 1873 (Andrew Forde & Bridget Forde; civil record has "father in America")
James, 1876 (James Greally & Kate Judge)
Ellen, 1878 (James Freeman & Bridget Judge)

Note: Bridget was the daughterof Michael Forde, dec'd, of Ballindrehid. Patrick was the son of James Caulfield of Bekan.

Sarah Forde & James O'Malley
m. June 1867 (John Fitzmaurice & Elizabeth Fitzmaurice)
Mary Susan, Sept. 1874 (Peter Flanagan & Anne Coffey)
Austin, Augt. 1878 (William & Ellen O'Malley)

Note: Sarah was the daughter of Charles Forde of Ballyhaunis. James was the son of Pat O'Malley of Ballyhaunis. Residence after marriage needs to be verified.

John Forde & Mary Harkin
Bridget, Oct. 1867 (civil record), Larganboy

Margaret, Sept. 1870 (Pat & Bridget Forde)
Mary, Dec. 1872 (Michael Hopkins & Bridget McGroak)
Ellen, Feb. 1874 (Judith Forde)

Catherine Forde & Edward Finn (Fynn)
m. Feb. 1868 (Patrick Finn & Bridget?)
Michael, July 1869 (civil record), Larganboy
James, Oct. 1871 (Martin Meath & Mary Forde)
Mary, 1874 (D. Moran & Ellen Forde) [record requires verification]
Edward, Augt. 1877 (Martin & Winifred Flynn)

Note: Catherine was the daughter of Jams Forde of Larganboy. Edward was
the son of Michael Finn of Larganboy.

John Forde & Mary Murray
John, June 1868 (Thomas Forde & Bridget Waldron), Bekan

John Forde & Catherine Moran,
Bridget, 1869 (Martin Duggan & Honor Cox), Bekan [record requires verification]

Bridget Forde & Thomas McDonnell
m. Feb. 1870 (Patrick Tague? & Catherine Forde), Bekan
Catherine, Augt.1872 (Thomas Kearns & Catherine Forde)

Note: Bridget was the daughter of Pat Forde, dec'd., of Coolnafarna. Thomas
was the son of Thomas McDonnell, dec'd., of Brickeens.

Patrick Forde & Anne Waldron
m. Feb. 1870 (Thomas Nolan & Ellen Waldron), Reask
Mary, Apr. 1872 (Michael Forde & Mary Grogan)
Margaret, July 1873 (Michael Waldron & Mary Niland)
Ellen, May 1875 (Owen Nolan & Ellen Forde)
Anne, March 1877 (James Lowry & Mary Morley)
Catherine, Jan. 1878 (Larry Grogan & Catherine Forde)
Ellen, Sept. 1880 (civil record)
Michael, May 1883 (civil record)
Bridget, July 1885 (John Cunnane & Bridget Forde)

Note: Patrick was the son of Michael Forde of Reask. Anne was the daughter of James Waldron & Mary Niland of Bunnadober, Bekan. She was the sister of Michael Waldron who married Anne Forde in 1876.

Bridget Forde & Thomas Lyons
m. March 1870 (Martin Lyons & Bridget Forde), Larganboy
Michael, Sept. 1871 (James & Mary Forde)
Mary, Oct. 1874 (Michael & Sara Forde)

Note: Bridget was the daughter of Michael Forde of Larganboy. Thomas was the son of Martin Lyons of Larganboy.

Bridget Forde & John Cunniff
m. Feb. 1872 (Pat Finn & Winifred Finn), Reask
Margaret, Feb. 1873 (James & Mary Forde)
Thomas, Jan. 1874 (civil record), Coogue
Mary, 1877 (Michael Forde & Mary Grogan)

Note: Bridget was the daughter of James Forde of Larganboy. John was the son of Thomas Cunniff, dec'd., of Coogue.

Anne Forde & Michael Carney
m. March 1873 (Michael Ford & Mary Forde), Bekan

Note: Anne was the daughter of Michael Forde of Larganboy. Michael was the son of Andrew Carney of Coogue.

Denis Forde & Ellen Fitzmaurice
m. March 1873 (Thomas Rattigan & Bridget Kenny), Ballyhaunis
Charles Patrick, Feb. 1874 (James O'Malley & Mary Fitzmaurice)
Denis Austin, Augt. 1875 (Michael Mulkinney? & Honor Fitzmaurice)
Elizabeth, March 1877 (Pat Freely & Honora Fitzmaurice)
Denis, March 1879 (Thomas & Cecilia Lyons)
Patrick, March 1881 (John Fitzmaurice & Anne O'Malley)
Mary, March 1883 (Pat & Honora Forde)
Denis, Jan. 1886 (? Golden & M. Godfrey)

Note: Denis, described as a "publican," was the son of Charles Forde, dec'd., of Ballyhaunis. Ellen was the daughter of Patrick Fitzmaurice, dec'd., of Ballyhaunis.

James Forde & Mary Hopkins
m. March 1874 (James Forde & Oney Forde), Larganboy
Michael, Augt 1877 (Bernard & Mary Kenny)
Hugh, Dec. 1884 (civil record)
Catherine, Feb. 1893 (Patrick & Mary Lyons)
Daniel, Oct. 1897 (Pat Fahy & B. Lyons)

Note: James was the son of Michael Forde, dec'd., of Larganboy. Mary was the daughter of James Hopkins of Larganboy.

Bridget Forde & John Cunnane
m. March 1875 (William Cunnane & Anne Forde)

Note: Bridget was the daughter of Michael Forde of Reask. John was the son of Mathias Cunnane of Coogue.

Catherine Forde & Eugene Nolan
Michael, Feb.1876 (Martin Nolan & Anne Forde), Bekan

Note: this may be the same family listed above as Catherine Forde & Owen Nolan.

Anne Forde & Michael Waldron
m. March 1876 (Michael Waldron & Ellen Forde)
James Patrick, March 1877 (Pat Forde & Ellen Lyons), Clagnagh
Michael & Mary, Jan. 1879 (John Waldron & Ellen Forde;? & Bridget Hunt)
Patrick, Apr. 1881 (Michael & Cecilia Waldron)
John, Dec. 1882 (Dominick Nolan & Mary Mulhearn)
Thomas, Apr. 1886 (Owen & Kate Nolan)
Richard, Sept. 1891 (Michael & Mary Waldron)

Note: Anne was the daughter of Michael Forde of Reask. Michael was the son of James Waldron, dec'd., of Clagnagh.

Honoria Forde & Patrick Smyth (Smith)

m. Dec. 1876 (John Joseph Dillon & Bridget Kelly), Churchfield
John Thomas, Sept. 1877 (Andrew Forde & Bridget Smyth)
Catherine, Oct. 1878 (John & Bridget K-?)
Bridget, June 1881 (Joseph? & Mary Grogan)
Michael, Nov. 1882 (John Reily & Mary Ganley), Ballyhaunis
Patrick, Apr. 1884 (John & Bridget Kelly)
Anne, Oct. 1885 (Andrew Forde & Bridget Kelly), Carrowluggaun
James, Apr. 1887 (Pat Smyth & Mary Dunbar)
Mary, Oct.1888 (civil record)
Honor, Jan.1892 (Michael Smyth & Lizzie Smyth)

Note: Honoria was the daughter of Andrew Forde of Churchfield. Patrick was the son of John Smyth of Ballyhaunis.

Mary Forde & Patrick Flynn
m. Jan. 1877 (John Moran & Catherine Moran), Clooncrim
John, Nov. 1877 (civil record)

Note: Mary was the daughter of John Forde of Clooncrim. Patrick was the son of Michael Flynn, dec'd., of Clooncrim.

Elizabeth Forde & John Charles Fitzmaurice
m. Feb. 1877 (Dominick Andrew Cullinane & Maria Fitzmaurice), Ballyhaunis

Note: Elizabeth was the daughter of Charles Forde of Ballyhaunis. John Charles was the son of Patrick Fitzmaurice, carpenter, of Ballyhaunis.

Patrick Forde & Bridget Duggan
m. Apr. 1877 (Thomas Duggan & Maggie Duggan)

Note: Patrick was the son of Thady Forde, dec'd., of Coolnafarna. Bridget was the daughter of James Duggan, dec'd., of Lissaniska.

Patrick Forde & Catherine Bryne
m. Feb. 1878 (Martin Boyle & Margaret Gavan?), Knock Parish

Note: Patrick, age 30, was the son of John Forde of Moureen. Catherine, age 25, was the daughter of John Byrne of Wingfield.

Catherine Forde & James Waldron
m. March 1878 (Patt Waldron & Margaret Kirrane)

Note: Catherine, age 26, was the daughter of Timothy Forde of Coolnafarna. James, age 28, was the son of Patrick Waldron of Coolnafarna.

Honor Forde & Pat Finn
m. Feb. 1880 (Austin Finn & Mary Forde?), Bekan

Note: Honor was the daughter of Pat Forde of Larganboy. Pat was the son of Austin Finn of Erriff. The name was spelled Fynn.

Mary Forde & Edward Morley
m. Jan. 1882 (Edward Currigan? & Bridget Murphy)
Edward, Feb. 1901 (Martin & Ellen Morris)

Note: Mary was the daughter of John Forde of Cloontumper. Edward was the son of Edward Morley of Cloonbulban.

Mary Forde & Thomas Kelly
m. Jan. 1883 (Martin Kelly & Mary Kelly), Bohauns

Note: Mary, age 23, was the daughter of John Forde of Bohauns. Thomas was the son of James Kelly of "The Woods," Kiltimaugh.

Ellen Forde & Thomas Caulfield
m. March 1883 (John Caulfield & Bridget Forde)

Note: Ellen, age 24, was the daughter of James Forde, dec'd., of Larganboy. Thomas, age 22, was the son of Martin Caulfield, dec'd., of Coogue.

Michael Forde & Jane Lyons
m. March 1883 (Thomas & Bridget Kelly) Churchpark

Note: Michael was the son of Andrew Ford of Churchpark. Jane Lyons was the daughter of Michael Lyons of Churchpark.

James Forde & Mary Forde
m. May 1884 (Michael & Julia Forde), Larganboy
James, Sept. 1885 (Pat Forde & Julia Forde)
Thomas, Jan. 1887 (T. Feeny & M. McHugh)
Julia, Jan. 1889 (M. Finn & Margaret Carney)
Patrick, Feb. 1891 (civil record)
Bridget, Feb. 1893 (William Forde & Bridget Carney)
Patrick & Martin, Dec. 1894 (civil record)
Mary Ellen, March 1897 (civil record)
Kate & Maggie, Jan. 1900 (Ed & Kate Finmore?; James & Mary Rein?)
Norah, Oct. 1902 (Thomas & Honoria Forde)

Note: James was the son of James Forde, dec'd., of Larganboy. Mary was the daughter of Thomas Forde, dec'd., of Reask.

Thomas Forde & Mary Hunt
m. May 1884 (Michael Tully & Kate Fitzmaurice), Derrynacong
Bridget, Jan. 1888 (Hugh Hunt & Maggie Tully)
Mary Ellen, May 1889 (Kate Waldron)
Patrick, Augt. 1892 (Pat & Bridget Fitzmaurice)
Delia & Kate, Dec. 1893 (Michael Hunt & Mary Fitzmaurice; Pat Tully & Mary Waldron)
John, Jan. 1896 (John & Celia Waldron)

Note: Thomas was the son of Patrick Forde, dec'd., & Bridget Freeman of Derrynacong. Mary Hunt was the daughter of Patrick Hunt, dec'd., & Bridget Fitzmaurice of Laughil, Co. Roscommon.

Ellen Forde & John Murray
m. Feb. 1885 (Pat Hopkins & Bridget Forde), Island

Note: Ellen, age 28, was the daughter of Thomas Forde of Island. John, age 37, was the son of James Murray of Erriff.

Bridget Forde & Patrick Hopkins
m. March 1888 (Roger Bones & Mary Murphy), Larganboy East

Note: Bridget, age 42, was the daughter of John Forde of Island. Patrick, age 44, was the son of Michael Hopkins, dec'd., of Larganboy East.

Thomas Forde & Bridget Judge
m. March 1889 (James Veasy & Jane Judge) Annagh Parish

Note: Thomas, age 33, was the son of Michael Forde of Reask. Bridget, age 25, was the daughter of Pat Judge of Curries.

Mary Forde & Patrick Kedian
m. May 1889 (Thomas Neary & Bridget Forde), Bekan
Thomas, March 1890 (civil record)
Mary, March 1893 (civil record)

Note: Mary was the daughter of Pat Forde, dec'd., of Larganboy. Patrick was the son of John Kedian of Moneymore. Mary died in March 1893, age given as 34. The child Mary also died in March 1893.

Bridget Forde & Andrew Ganley
m. March 1890 (Pat Killeen & Anne Forde), Bekan

Note: Bridget was the daughter of Pat Forde of Larganboy. Andrew was the son of Luke Ganley of Carrowneden.

Bridget Forde & Michael Murphy
m. March 1890 (Thomas Freely & Mary Ann Forde), Annagh

Note: Bridget was the daughter of William Forde of Coolnafarna. Michael was the son of Myles Murphy, dec'd., of Gorteen.

Daniel Forde & Maggie Lyons
m. Apr. 1890 (Pat Fahey & Bridget Lyons), Bekan

Note: Daniel was the son of Pat Forde of Larganboy. Maggie was the daughter of Michael Lyons of Knocknafola?

Thomas Forde & Julia Atkinson
Thomas, Feb. 1893 (Pat Atkinson & Rose Atkinson) Breen, Knock
Bridget, Dec. 1897 (civil record), Ballyhowly

Matthew Forde & Honoria Higgins
m. March 1894 (Thomas O'Brien & Ellen Higgins, Bohauns
Mary, Jan. 1896 (Martin Higgins & Ellen Higgins)
Anne, Jan. 1900 (civil record)
John Thomas, Nov. 1901 (civil record)
Michael, Sept. 1903 (civil record)
James, May 1905 (civil record)

Note: Matthew, age 26, was the son of John Forde of Bohauns. Honoria, age 19, was the daughter of John Higgins of Killeen?

Anne Forde & Patrick Grogan
m. June 1896 (Michael Lyons & Norah Hunt)

Note: Anne, age 25, was the daughter of Thomas Forde, dec'd., of Larganboy West. Patrick, age 29, was the son of Laurence Grogan of Larganboy West.

Mary Forde & James McDonnell
m. Jan. 1897 (Malachy Tarpy & Kate Forde)

Note: Mary was the daughter of Thomas Forde of Larganboy. James was the son of Austin McDonnell of Lecarrow.

Thomas Forde & Catherine Cuniffe
m. March 1897 (Andrew Forde & Maggie Cuniffe), Reask
Ellen, March 1899 (John Cuniffe & Rose Duffy)
Anne, Augt. 1900 (Thomas Brown & Margaret Nolan)
Patrick, Feb. 1902 (Michael & Bridget Forde)

Note: Thomas, age 40, widower, was the son of Michael Forde, dec'd., of Reask. Catherine, age 30, was the daughter of James Cuniffe of Liscat.

Thomas Forde & Bridget Lyons
m. Nov. 1897 (John Waldron & Anne Higgins), Derrynacong
Anne, Sept. 1898 (James Waldron & Catherine Bones)
Norah, Jan. 1900 (Edward Lyons & Mary Higgins)
Rose, Dec. 1901 (Michael Lyons & Mary Ellen Forde)
Agnes, Dec. 1903 (Hubert Forde & Catherine Lyons)

Note: Thomas, widower of Mary Hunt, was the son of Patrick Forde, dec'd., & Bridget Freeman of Derrynacong. Bridget was the daughter of Edward Lyons & Catherine Bones of Larganboy.

Andrew Forde & Mary Kilduff
m. circa 1897 (Martin Morley & Honor Tigue), Ballindrehid [record requires verification]

Note: Andrew was the son of John Forde & Mary Henry. Mary was from Wingfield, Knock.

Jane Forde & Austin McDonnell
m. Nov. 1898 (Roger McDonnell & Mary Killion), Churchpark

Jane (nee Lyons) was the widow of Michael Forde and the daughter of Michael Lyons of Churchpark. Austin was the son of Owen McDonnell of Churchpark.

Andrew Forde & Norah Langhan
m. Feb. 1901 (Michael Forde & Kate Langhan), Reask
Thomas Patrick, March 1902 (James & Kate Langhan)

Note: Andrew was the son of Thomas Forde of Reask. Norah was the daughter of James Langhan of Cullentragh.

Mary Anne Forde & Peter Burke
m. Apr. 1901 (Patrick Reilly & Kate Morley), Knock Parish

Note: Mary Anne was the daughter of William Forde of Srah. Peter was the son of Michael Burke of [illegible].

Elizabeth Forde & James Morley
m. Apr. 1901 (? & Delia Ford), Knock Parish

Note: Elizabeth was the daughter of Pat Forde of Churchfield. James was the son of Pat Morley of Ballyfarman?

James Forde & Bridget Flatley
m. Jan. 1902 (Thomas Grogan & Maggie Flatley), Hazelhill

Thomas Michael, Dec. 1902 (civil record)
James Patrick, March 1906 (civil record)

Note: James was the son of Thomas Forde of Hazelhill. Bridget was the daughter of Peter Flatley of Carramore, Knock.

James Forde & Mary Egan
m. Jan 1902 Richard Egan & Bridget McKenna) Tuam cathedral?
Patrick, March 1904 (civil record)
John, Feb. 1906 (Peter Lyons & Mary Quirk), Ballyhaunis
Thomas, June 1909 (Patrick Quirk & Elizabeth Clarke)

Note: James, described as a "musician," was the son of James Forde, dec'd., of Tierboy Road, Galway. Mary was the daughter of Thomas Egan of Tierboy Road.

Catherine Forde & John Flatley
m. Jan. 1903 (Patrick Caulfield & Lizzie Carney), Bekan

Note: Catherine was the daughter of Andrew Forde of Bekan. John was the son of Martin Flatley of Brackloon.

Patrick Forde & Catherine Hopkins
m. Feb. 1904 (John Hopkins & Rose Hopkins), Bekan

Note: Patrick was the son of John Forde of Larganboy. Catherine was the daughter of Patrick Hopkins of Larganboy.

Hubert Forde & Catherine Carney
m. Apr. 1904 (James Finn & Mary Caulfield), Larganboy

Note: Hubert was the son of Patrick Forde of Larganboy. Catherine was the daughter of John Carney of Shunnaghmeel?, Knock Parish.

John Forde & Mary Byrne
m. March 1906 (James Hunt & Norah Byrne), Bekan

Note: John was the son of William Forde of Reask. Mary was the daughter of John Byrne of Derrymore.

Martin Forde & Bridget Gannon
m. Apr. 1908 (James Connaughton & Sarah Anne Costello)

Note: Martin was the son of Thomas Forde of Carrow Beg. Bridget was the son of Thomas Gannon of Killknock.

John Forde & Catherine Fahey
m. June 1908 (Thomas Forde of Ballindrehid & Delia Regan), Ballindrehid

Note: John was the son of John Forde of Ballindrehid. Catherine was the daughter of Pat Fahey of Ballinclogher, Aghamore.

Thomas Forde & Mary Grealy
m. Apr. 1910 (James Forde of Ballindrehid & Mary Grealy), Union St., Ballyhaunis
Mary Kate, March 1911 (Timothy Freeman & Anne Gilmore)
John Patrick, Jan. 1912 (civil record)
Margaret, Apr. 1913 (John Caulfield & Catherine Forde)
Andrew, May 1914 (civil record)
Bridget, May 1916 (civil record)
Mary, Augt. 1917 (civil record)

Note: Thomas, described as a "boot maker," was the son of John Forde of Ballindrehid. Mary was the daughter of John Greally of Shanvaghera, Knock Parish.

Bridget Forde & Thomas Johnston
m. March 1912 (Martin Higgins & Bridget Lyons), Reask
James, July 1913 (Patrick Finn & Winifred Finn)
Patrick, March 1914 (Michael Forde & Winifred Johnston)
Thomas, Dec. 1915 (Thomas Murphy & Bridget Forde)

Note: Bridget was the daughter of Pat Forde & Anne Waldron of Reask. Thomas, age 26, was the son of James Johnston & Winifred Finn of Reask.

Michael Forde & Margaret Murray
m. March 1913 (John Cunnane & Kate Murray), Reask
Anne, March 1914 (Thomas Johnston & Bridget Forde)
Patrick, May 1915 (John Cunnane & Elizabeth Byrne)
Elizabeth, July 1916 (James Murphy & Catherine Cunnane)

Note: Michael, age 29, was the son of Patrick Forde & Anne Waldron of Reask. Margaret was the daughter of William Murray of Lissaniska.

Teresa Forde & Michael Grealy, Ballyhaunis
Michael Martin, Sept. 1914 (Andrew Grealy & Susan Forde), Ballyhauns
Michael, Sept. 1920 (Andrew Grealy & Susan Forde)


Civil record of deaths (townlands and informants are in parentheses)

Julia (Judith) Forde, Sept. 1865, 75, widow, (Ballyhaunis, Peter Mullowny)
Charles Forde, June 1866, 75, (Churchfield, Denis Forde) [record requires verification]
Austin Forde, June, 1866, 7, (Larganboy, Thomas Forde, father)
Anne Forde, June 1867, 1, (Larganboy) [record requires verification]
Thomas Forde, Jan. 1870, 55, married, (Reask, Thomas Waldron)
John Forde, Feb. 1878, 76, widower, (Island, Bridget Forde)
Michael Forde, July, 1878, 51, married, (Reask, James Murray of Coogue)
Honoria Forde, July 1878, 70, widow, (Ballindrehid, Mary Ford)
John Forde, June 1879, 55, married, (Larganboy, Mary Forde)
Ellen Forde, Dec. 1879, 78, widow, (Larganboy, James Forde)
John Forde, July 1880, 70, married, (Clooncrim, Bridget Flynn)
Catherine Forde, May 1881, 60, widow, (Lissaniska, Pat Culliney of Tawnaghmore)
Daniel Forde, Nov. 1881, one day, (Larganboy, Bridget Lyons)
Jane Forde, July 1882, 70, publican's widow, (Ballyhaunis, Bridget O'Neil)
Mary Forde, Oct. 1882, 76, married, (Island, Ellen Forde)
Mary Forde, June 1883, one day, (Larganboy, Thomas Forde, father)
Patrick Forde, Augt. 1883, 60, widower, (Larganboy, Mary Forde, daughter)
Michael Forde, Augt. 1884, 66, married, (Reask, Ann Forde, daughter)
Andrew Forde, Feb.1885, 69, bachelor, (Ballindrehid, John Forde, nephew)
Patrick Forde, Feb. 1885, three months, (Coolnafarna, Bridget Forde, mother)
Patrick Forde, May 1885, 40, (Coolnafarna, Bridget Forde, wife)
Bridget Forde, Jan. 1886, 56, widow, (Reask, Michael Forde, son)
Mary Forde, March 1887, 60, widow, (Reask, John Cunnane, son-in-law)
Bridget Forde, Apr. 1888, 19, (Reask, Mary Forde, sister)
Thomas Forde, Dec. 1888, 84, widower, (Island, Michael Waldron, son-in-law)
Andrew Forde, Feb. 1889, 68 widower, (Carrownluggan, Pat Smith, son-in-law)
Andrew Forde, Sept. 1889, 32, single, (Larganboy, Thomas Forde, brother)

Mary Forde, Augt. 1890, 65, (Cloontumper, John Forde, husband)
John Forde, Dec. 1890, 56, (Larganboy, Judy Forde, wife)
Mary Forde, June 1892, 85, widow, (Coolnafarna, Bridget Forde, granddaughter)
Patrick Forde, Augt. 1892, 62, married, (Churchfield, Elizabeth Forde, daughter)
Michael Forde, Sept. 1892, 46, married, (Churchpark, James Lyons, brother-in-law)
James Forde, May 1893, 19, (Larganboy, Julia Forde, mother)
Ellen Forde, July 1895, 40, (Ballyhaunis, Denis Forde, husband)
Bridget Forde, July 1895, 28 days, (Ballyhaunis, Denis Forde, father)
Thomas Forde, Dec. 1895, 88, (Larganboy, Judy Forde, wife)
John Forde, Jan. 1896, 48, single, (Island, Bridget Forde, sister, of Larganboy)
Patrick Forde, March 1896, 73, (Larganboy, Anne Forde, wife)
Bridget Forde, June 1896, 31, (Reask, Thomas Forde, husband)
Mary Forde, Apr. 1897, 42, (Derrynacong, Thomas Forde, husband)
John Forde, Sept. 1897, 1, (Derrynacong, Thomas Forde, father)
Kate Forde, March 1898, 44, single, (Reask, Anna Henderson, sister)
John Forde, Nov. 1899, 67, widower, (Cloontumper, Edward Morley, son-in-law)
Honor Forde, Apr. 1901, 65, (Bekan, Andrew Forde, husband)
Annie Forde, Nov. 1901, 2, (Bohauns, Bridget McNicholas, aunt)
Mary Forde, Apr. 1902, 70, widow, (Derrinaco?, Castlerea workhouse)
Mary Forde, Sept. 1902, 77, married, (Bohauns, Ellen Stanton, sister-in-law)
Thomas Forde, Augt. 1903, two weeks, (Reask, Thomas Forde, father)
Mary Forde, June 1904, 11, (Reask, Mary Forde, sister)
John Forde, March 1905, three days, (Larganboy, Patrick Forde, farther)
Patrick Forde, Nov. 1906, 4, (Reask, Delia Forde, sister)
Margaret Forde, Augt. 1907, 81, (Hazelhill, Thomas Forde, husband)
John Forde, Apr. 1908, 79, widower, (Bohauns, Mary Forde grand-daughter)
James Forde, Dec. 1909, 68, married, (Larganboy, Patrick Forde, son)
Mary Forde, Jan. 1911, 78, widow, (Larganboy, Anne Grogan, daughter)
Thomas Forde, May 1911, 96, widower, (Hazelhill, Bridget Forde, daughter-in-law)
Anne Forde, July 1911, 67, (Reask, Patrick Forde, husband)
Margaret Forde, Jan. 1912, 69, (Coolnafarna, William Forde, husband)
Patrick Forde, June 1912, 74, widower, (Reask, Michael Forde, son)
Bridget Forde, Feb. 1915, 87, widower (Reask, Norah Forde, daughter-in-law)
William Forde, Sept. 1915, 78, married, (Laughil, William Forde, son)
Margaret Forde, Apr. 1916, 75, widow, (Laughil, William Forde, son)
James Forde, Sept. 1916, 58, (Island, Maria Forde, wife)
Aileen Forde, Sept. 1917, one month, (Ballyhaunis, Mary Ford, mother)
Bridget Forde, March 1920, 54, (Derrynacong, Thomas Forde, husband)

<u>Inscription – Friary Cemetery, The Abbey, Ballyhaunis</u>

John Forde, Ballyhaunis, died 3 January 1808, age 34
His wife, Margaret, died 26 Apr., 1826, age 58

Erected by their son Patrick Forde of Ballyhaunis.

Also in grave, Dan Forde of Larganboy, died 6 August 1926
[72 years, married, brother-in-law Patrick Lyons of Carrowkeel informant]


<u>Other Friary Graves</u>

Julia Forde, died 11 Feb. 1815 [record requires verification]

Thomas Forde of Reask, age 51, died 7 Jan. 1871
His wife Bridget, age 86, died 25 Feb. 1915

Bridget Waldron Forde, died 25 Feb. 1915

Margaret Forde & Matthew Waldron
Matthew died 26 March 1826, Island

# Freeman Families in the Vicinity of Ballyhaunis in the 19<sup>th</sup> Century

The surname Freeman derives from the Irish *O Saorthaigh* or from *Mac anTSaoir*, which translates as "descendent (or son) of the laborer." Another, perhaps older, Anglicized version of the name was "Seery."

The Freeman surname is more firmly localized in Aghamore Parish than in Annagh, Bekan and Kiltullagh Parishes.

<u>Annagh & Bekan Parishes - Griffith's Valuation – 1856</u>

Andrew Freeman, Gorteen, Annagh Parish

Thomas Freeman, Gorteen, Annagh Parish

Martin Freeman & Luke Hansboro, Bohogerawer, Bekan Parish

Martin Freeman & Luke Hansboro, Bracklaghboy, Bekan Parish

Annagh & Bekan Parish Registers

John Freeman & Anne Beanis (Bones?)
Anne, 1835?, Bekan Parish [record requires verification]

Bridget Freeman & John Lyons
John, 1836 (Bridget Jeffers & Michael Hunt), Bekan Parish
Peter, c.1840 (John Swift) [record requires verification]
Patrick, 1845 (John McHale & Mary McHale)

Martin Freeman (Seery) & Bridget Hansburgh (Hansboro)
m. March 1836 (James? & Mary Filan?), Bracklaghboy
Andrew, Dec. 1837 (Luke & Rose Hansbro)
Mary, 1840 (Thomas & Rose Hansbro) [record requires verification]
Michael, 1843 (Michael? & Peggy Hunt)
Kate, March 1848 (Patrick Waldron & Rose Flynn)
Bridget, Feb. 1852 (Michael Walsh & Bridget Dowd)

Michael Freeman & Catherine Durr (Dunn?)
Catherine, Dec. 1844 (John McGreal & Ellen Brennan), Bekan Parish
Mary, 1846 (Thady & Mary Freeman)

Mary Freeman & John Deasy
Mary, July 1852 (Bridget Freeman), Annagh Parish

Bridget Freeman & Patrick Forde
Michael, June 1853 (John Freely? & Catherine Dyer), Derrynacong
Thomas, July 1856 (Henry & Anne Hamrock)
Hubert, June 1858 (Mary Hunt)

Sabina Freeman & John Dyer
m. Nov. 1856 (John Nary & Ellen Waldron), Bekan Parish

Catherine Freeman & Austin Lyons
Thomas, Nov. 1856 (Patrick Kilkenny & Mary Kilkenny), Ballyhaunis
Bridget & Susan, March 1861 (Patrick Lyons & Mary Lyons)
Anne, Augt. 1862 (Bernard Lyons & Bridget Lyons)
Michael, March 1864 (James Lyons & Mary Lyons)

James Augustine, May 1866 (James Lyons & Sabina Lyons)
Catherine & Bridget, June 1868 (Michl Kilkenny & Mary Murray; Pat Lyons & Margt. Brown)
Teresa, Augt. 1870 (civil record)
James Augustine, Feb. 1872 (Pat Fitzmaurice & Bridget?)

Note: Austin Lyons was described as a "tailor." He died May 1893, age given as 76. Catherine died May 1897, age given as 68. Informant for both was daughter Mary Hannah Jordan. Baptism and marriage records have not been located for Mary Hannah.

? Freeman & Patrick Kelly
Bridget, 1856?, Annagh Parish [record requires verification]

Bridget Freeman & Patrick Comber
Michael, 1860 (Michael Comber & Catherine Freeman), Greenwood
Catherine, 1863 (Mary Freeman)

Patrick died March 1883, age given as 55. (Honny Freeman informant.) Bridget died Nov. 1897, age given as 65. (Daughter-in-law Catherine Comber informant.)

Thomas Freeman & Mary Glavy
Michael, Sept. 1864 (civil record), Gorteen
Mary, Feb. 1870 (James & Bridget Royan)
John, May 1867 (civil record)
Bridget, Dec. 1872 (Pat Naree? & Mary Kedian)
Thomas, July 1878 (Daniel Frehily & Ellen Brennan)

Note: Thomas Freeman was described as a "tailor." Thomas Freeman, baptized in 1878, immigrated to the United States, possibly in Apr. 1900. He died in Plainfield, New Jersey, in Oct. 1958. He married Mary Anne Rafferty, the daughter of Thomas Rafferty & Bridget Ryan. She was baptized in Loughglynn, Co. Roscommon in June 1877. Mary died in New Jersey in Nov. 1966.

Michael and John never married. Michael immigrated to the United States. Mary married a man named McCann, likely in the United States. Bridget married Thomas Lyons (see below).

Anne Freeman & William Carroll
Mary, Sept. 1865 (Thomas Freeman & Mary Cunnane), Ballindrehid
Catherine, 1868 (James Freeman & Catherine Freeman) [record needs to be
verified]

Note: Anne was the daughter of Michael Freeman of Ballindrehid. William
Carroll likely died in 1869, age given as 34.

Honoria Freeman & Michael Hoban, Annagh Parish
Michael, Feb. 1867 (Martin Freeman & Catherine Freeman) [record requires
verification]

Mary Freeman & Peter Healy
m. Feb. 1870 (Peter Healy & Honor Freeman), Corraun, Annagh Parish
John, May 1871 (civil record)

Note: Mary was the daughter of Thomas Freeman, dec'd., of Gorteen. Peter,
described as a widower, was the son of Denis Healy, dec'd., of Corraun.

Catherine Freeman & Thomas Salmon
m. Feb. 1870 (Thomas Salmon & Mary Hunt), Bohogerawer
Patrick, Nov. 1870 (James Malloy & Anne? Salmon)
Mary, Jan. 1876 (James & Anne Carney)
Thomas, Oct. 1877 (Mark & Rose Ansbro)
Michael Edward, 1880 (Pat Mulhern & Anne Carney)
John Joseph, Oct. 1882 (Thomas Carney & Anne Carney)
James Martin, 1884 (Pat Salmon & Kate Kenny)
Catherine, Sept. 1890 (James Costello & Bridget Salmon)

Note: Catherine Freeman was the daughter of Martin Freeman of Bracklaghboy.
Thomas was the son of Thomas Salmon, dec'd., of Cloon -? There is a
March 1923 death record for Thomas Salmon, age 84, in Carrownanaght?
(Informant was son, Thomas.) John Joseph died in March 1883.

Anne Carroll (nee Freeman) & Michael Gaynor
m. March 1870 (Michael Freeman & Mary Carroll), Ballindrehid
Anne, Augt. 1876 (John & Mary Jane McGual?)

Note: Anne Carroll was the daughter of Michael Freeman of Gorteen. She died, age 55, in Nov. 1899. Michael Gayner, described as a "constable," was the son of Patrick Gaynor, dec'd., of Loughglynn, Co. Roscommon. He died, age given as 90, in Apr. 1893. (Informant was daughter Anne.)

Michael Freeman & Catherine Judge
m. Feb. 1877 (James Mannion & Catherine Cunnane), Ballindrehid
Mary, Nov. 1878 (Thomas Freeman & Anne Burke)
James, July 1881 (John Fitzmaurice & Bridget Judge)
Michael, May 1884 (Pat Freeman & Catherine Burke)
Bridget, July 1886 (Thomas Forde & Sarah Fitzmaurice)
John Thomas, May 1888 (Michael Forde & Kate Judge)
Patrick, June 1890 (civil record)
Timothy, March 1892 (A. Burke & Ellen Burke)
Francis, Sept. 1893 (Thomas Grealy & Mary Forde)
Joseph, Jan. 1895 (civil record, Mary Anne Freeman present)
Catherine Josephine, Feb. 1898 (Patrick Forde & Ellen Caulfield)
Margaret Henrietta, Dec. 1900 (Thomas Forde & Bridget Waldron)

Note: Michael was the son of James Freeman of Ballinacostello, Aghamore. Catherine was the daughter of Patrick Judge & Mary Forde of Ballindrehid.

Bridget Freeman & Thomas Lyons
m. July 1911 (Martin Hunt & Mary Caulfield), Gorteen
John Martin, Oct. 1912 (civil record)
Nora, Dec. 1913 (Anthony Lyons & Nora Lyons)

Note: Bridget was the daughter of Thomas Freeman of Gorteen. Thomas was the son of Thady Lyons of Scregg.

Catherine Freeman & Patrick Finn
m. Feb. 1920 (Austin Kenny & Margaret Freeman)

Note: Catherine was the daughter of Michael Freeman & Catherine Judge of Ballindrehid. Patrick was the son of Patrick Finn of Cappagh.

Timothy Freeman & Mary McNicholas
m. Feb. 1926 (James Malley & Mary Jeffers)

Note: Timothy was the son of Michael Freeman & Catherine Judge of Ballindrehid. Mary was the daughter of Michael McNicholas & Ellen McLoughlin of Shunagh., Knock. She was baptized in August 1893.

John Freeman & Katie Caulfield
m. Dec. 1926 (Patrick Waldron & Annie Freeman)

Note: John, age 29 and described as "Post," was the son of John Freeman of Ballyhaunis. Katie was the daughter of Thomas Caulfield of Ballyhaunis.

Civil record of deaths (townlands and informants are in parentheses)

Andrew Freeman, Jan. 1869, 60, married, (Gorteen, Honoria Freeman)
Bridget Freeman, March 1870, 80, marital status uncertain, (Gorteen, Thomas Freeman)
Martin Freeman, Sept. 1870, 60, widower, (Bracklaghboy, Catherine Salmon)
Margaret Freeman, Apr. 1873, 65, widow, (Sellernane, Pat Egan)
Bridget Freeman, Nov. 1878, 58, widow, (Meeltran, Thos. Freeman, Ballinacostello)
Thomas Freeman, June 1879, 45, married, (Gorteen, Michael Freeman)
Catherine Freeman, July 1881, 40, married, (Gorteen, Honny Freeman)
Thady Freeman, Jan. 1887, 60, married, (Meeltran, Catherine Freeman, niece, Ballindre.)
Mary Freeman, June 1898, 62, widow, (Gorteen, Thomas Freeman, son)
Honoria Freeman, June 1902, 45, single, (Gorteen, Ned Freeman, brother)
Bridget Freeman, Feb. 1903, 77, widow, (Meeltran, Claremorris workhouse)
James Freeman, March 1903, 21, single, (Ballindrehid, Catherine Freeman, mother)
Michael Freeman, Jan. 1904, 19, single, (Ballindrehid, Catherine Freeman, mother)
Thomas Freeman, Nov. 1905, 25, married, (Ballinacostello, Thomas Freeman, father)
Edward Freeman, March 1911, 75, single, (Claremorris Workhouse)
John Freeman, Jan. 1915, 24, single, (Bracklaghboy, Michael Freeman, father)
Timothy Freeman, May 1931, 75, married, (Ballindrehid, Timothy Freeman, son)
Catherine Freeman, Dec. 1936, 77, widow, (Ballindrehid, Timothy Freeman, son)
John Freeman, July 1942, 75, single, (Gorteen, John Lyons, nephew)

Timothy Freeman, Feb. 1964, 71, married, (Ballindrehid, Mary Freeman, wife)
Ellen Freeman, March 1964, 79, widow, (Mountain, Mary Plunkett, daughter)


Kiltullagh Parish - Griffith's Valuation – 1856

Cormack Freeman, Cloonalough, Kiltullagh Parish


Kiltullagh Parish Register

Mary Freeman & Bernard Grogan
m. Jan. 1846 (Edward Grogan & B. Dodd), Cloonalough
Bridget, Sept. 1849 (Cormack Freeman & Sarah Grogan)
Michael, July 1852 (D. Connor & Mary Grogan)
Thomas, Dec. 1853 (Thomas Greg? & Mary Fleming)
James, Dec. 1857? [record requires verification]
Bridget, Nov. 1863 (James & Bridget Grogan)
Michael, Oct. 1864 (Mary Jennings)
Catherine, Nov. 1865 (Michael Grogan & Mary McDemott)

Mary Freeman & Francis Grogan
Mary, Dec. 1846 (Ned Grogan & Befs? Dodd). Clough?

Note: the two records above may the same family.

Mary Freeman & John Fleming
John, Augt. 1865 (John Freeman? & Mary Kelly), Cloonfad

Anne Freeman & Edward Grogan
Sarah, Feb. 1866 (civil record), Cloonalough
Anne, Apr. 1868 (civil record)
Catherine, May 1870 (Michael & Mary Grogan)

Additional Kiltullagh Notes

The following individuals resided in Kiltullagh Parish in the early 1840s: Thomas Freeman and Cormack Freeman in Cloonalough and Hugh Freeman in Foxboro.

Aghamore Parish - Diocese of Tuam Marriage Records

Patrick Seery & Mary Costello
m. Feb. 1822 (John Jordan & Michael Curry)

Dominick Seary & Catherine Henry
m. Feb. 1823 (Austin Henry & Mary -)

Michael Seary & Mary Cosgrove
m. Feb. 1823 (John Seary & Peter Burke)

Catherine Seary & Michael Costello
m. Apr. 1823 (John Costello & John Seary)

Honor Searry & Andrew Folliard
m. Jan. 1827 (James Folliard & James Searry)

Aghamore Parish - Griffith's Valuation – 1856

Michael Freeman, Aghataharn

James Freeman, Ballinacostello
Thomas Freeman

Patrick Freeman, Barnahesker

James Freeman, Boleyboy
Thomas Freeman

Thomas Freeman, Cappagh

Thomas Freeman, Cartron North

John Freeman, Derrycashel

John Freeman, Falleighter
James Freeman

Patrick Freeman (John), Lismeegaun
Patrick Freeman (Larry)

Timothy Freeman, Meeltran

Aghamore Parish Registers

Mary Freeman & John Conlon (Connellon)
m. Feb. 1864 (James Caulfield & Catherine Kilkenny)
Margaret, June 1869 (Martin & Bridget Conlon), Cloongawnagh
Patrick, Jan. 1873 (Martin Healy & Bridget Forkan)

Note: Mary was the daughter of Patrick Freeman of Lismeegaun. John ws the son of Patrick Conlon of Cloongunagh?

Thomas Freeman & Catherine Carroll
Anne, July 1864 (Pat Morley & Ellen Freeman), Esker

Patrick Freeman & Catherine Lyons
John, July 1864 (T. Kilkenny & Anne Freeman), Esker
Edward, Nov. 1865 (Pat Freeman & Mary Lyons)
James, Sept. 1867 (civil record)

Anne Freeman & James Kelly
Thomas James, Oct. 1864 (John Freeman & Bridget Kelly), Rath
Mary Anne, Sept. 1866 (John Freeman & Mary?)
James, Nov. 1867 (Anthony & Bridget Caulfield)
Patrick, Jan, 1869 (Thomas Kelly & Mary Maguire)
Bridget, Sept. 1870 (John & Mary Freeman)
John, Oct. 1871 (James Freeman & Mary Bones)
Margaret, Jan. 1873 (Martin & Mary Freeman)

Ellen, Jan. 1874 (James Halloran & Bridget Beirne)

Biddy Freeman & Pat Roddy
Thomas, Dec. 1864 (James Freeman & Bridget Moraine), Kilmovee?

James Freeman & Mary Burke
Bridget, Jan. 1865 (William Freeman & Anne Burke), Ballinacostello
Margaret, Augt. 1870 (Thomas Freeman & Catherine Lohan)

Michael Freeman & Honor Boyle
John, Sept. 1865 (Martin Lyons & Mary Freeman), Aghataharn
Thomas, Augt. 1867 (civil record)
Honor, Dec. 1869 (John Scally & Mary Freeman)
Matthew, Jan. 1872 (Pat Boyle & Honor Morley)
James, Oct. 1875 (Michael Flanagan & Jane Akinson)

William Freeman & Mary Tarpey
Bridget, Dec. 1865 (Thady Freeman & Mary Tarpey), Ballinacostello
William, Augt. 1868 (Patrick Flanagan & Bridget Frehilly)
Mary, Jan. 1872 (Thady Freeman & Mary Lyons)
Thomas, Augt. 1873 (John Lyons & Bridget Fleming)

Martin Freeman & Bridget Costello
Thomas, July 1867 (civil record), Curraghsalla?

Patrick Freeman & Susan Caulfield
m. Jan. 1868 (John Freeman & Sarah Caulfield), Coogue

Note: Patrick, agd 24, was the sn of James Freeman of Reath? Susan, age 23, was the daughter of Michael Caulfield of Coogue.

Thomas Freeman & Mary Flanagan
m. Dec. 1868 (John Campbell & Fanny Flanagan), Knock Parish
Michael, Apr. 1869 (Michael & Mary Waldron), Woodfield

Note: Thomas was the son of Michael Freeman of Woodfield. Mary was the daughter of
John Flanagan of Woodfield.

Mary Freeman & Patrick Kilkenny
m. Jan. 1870 (Arthur Kilkenny & Anne Freeman)

Note: Mary, age 23, was the daughter of Michael Freeman of Woodfield. Thomas, age 24, was the son of Thomas Kilkenny of Falleighter.

Michael Freeman & Ellen Keane
m. Feb. 1871 (John Boyle & Bridget Keane)
Mary, Dec. 1871 (James Keane & Mary Grogan), Esker
Catherine, Dec. 1872 (John O'Brien & Mary Grogan)
Thomas, Dec. 1878 (Thomas & Mary Kane)
Bridget, Feb. 1880 (Michael Caulfield & Catherine Keane)

Note: Michael, age 24, was the son of James Freeman of Rath. Ellen, age 20, was the daughter of Thomas Keane of Esker.

Mary Freeman & Patrick Tighe
m. July 1871 (James Burke & Anne Freeman), Falleighter
Catherine, Oct. 1871 (James Halloran & Anne Freeman)
Bridget, Oct. 1872 (John Freeman & Bridget Stenson)
Patrick, Jan. 1874 (John Freeman & Mary Halloran)
Michael, Augt. 1875 (James & Jane Freeman)
Martin, Oct. 1877 (Austin Freeman & Mary Haloran), Rath

Note: Mary, age 24, was the daughter of James Freeman, location illegible. Patrick, age 24, was the son of James Tighe of Ballincloha?

Sara Freeman & Timothy Lavan
m. Feb. 1873 (Patrick Lavan & Mary Lyons)

Note: Sara, age 19, was the daughter of Thaddeus Freeman of Meeltran. Timothy, age 25, was the son of Thomas Lavan of Shanvaghera.

Simon Freeman & Anne Caulfield
m. Feb. 1873 (Ned Freeman & Rose Caulfield)
Thomas, Dec. 1877 (Thomas & Mary Freeman), Crossbeg
Anthony, Jan. 1880 (Pat & Honor Caulfield)

Note: Simon, age 23, was the son of Thomas Freeman of Cartron. Anne was the daughter of Anthony Caulfield of Coogue.

Catherine Freeman & John Grogan
m. Feb. 1874 (John Kilkenny & Mary Freeman), Falleighter

Note: Catherine, age 22, was the daughter of Michael Freeman of Cloonturk. John, age 27, was the son of Matthew Grogan, dec'd., of Falleighter.

Ellen Freeman & Michael Harrison
m. Feb. 1874 (Francis O'Grady & Catherine Freeman)

Note: Ellen, age 24, was the daughter of Thomas Freeman of Esker. Michael, age 28, was the son of Roger Harrison of Kilmore?

Anne Freeman & Thomas Mullowney
m. March 1874 (Pat & Kate Freeman)
Catherine, Oct. 1876 (Pat & Catherine Freeman), Esker

Note: Anne, age 21, was the daughter of Patrick Freeman of Esker. Thomas, age 22, was the son of Thomas Mullowney of Curryan.

Austin Freeman & Mary Tigue (Tighe)
m. Apr. 1876 (Martin Freeman & Mary Tigue), Falleighter
Mary Anne, Apr. 1877 (John & Anne Freeman)
Martin, March 1880 (Pat & Bridget Tighe)

John Freeman & Catherine Freeman
m. Feb. 1877 (Anthony Caulfield & Mary Freeman)
Thomas, Oct. 1878 (John & Catherine Grogan), Rath
Michael, Sept. 1893 (civil record), Esker

Mary Freeman & Pat Horan
m. 1878 (Mark Horan & Catherine Freeman), Esker
Thomas, Sept. 1879 (Edward & Anne Freeman)

Note: Mary was the daughter of Michael Freeman [record requires verification].

Margaret Freeman & James Carney
m. Jan. 1879 (John Carney & Margaret Carney)
Mary, Feb. 1880 (Pat Freeman & Mary Conlon), Lismeegaun

Margaret, age 21, was the daughter of Pat Freeman of Lismeegaun. James, age 30, was the son of John Carney of Lismeegaun.

Mary Freeman & Michael Deasy
m. March 1879 (James Caulfield & Honor C -?; Bridget Lowery informant)
Michael, Oct. 1880 (civil record), Cartron North

Note: no civil record found for this marriage.

Mary Freeman & John Burke
m. Feb. 1889 (Pat Tully & Honora Clarke)

Note: Mary, age 26, was the daughter of James Freeman of Aghataharn. John, age 32, was the son of Richard Burke of Cloghvoley.

Thady Freeman & Mary Bones
m. Apr. 1889 (Edward Freeman & Mary Snee)

Note: Thady was the son of John Freeman of Derrycashel. Mary was the daughter of Thomas Bones of Cloontarriff.

Honoria Freeman & Patrick Nolan
m. March 1894 (James Nolan & Mary Sealy)

Note: Honoria, age 21, was the daughter of Michael Freeman of Aghataharn. Patrick was the son of Hugh Nolan of Cloongawnagh.

Thomas Francis Freeman & Bridget Ganley
m. Feb. 1904 (Timothy Freeman & Mary Boyle)
Michael Joseph, Nov. 1904 (civil record)

Note: Thomas Francis was the son of Thomas Freeman of Ballinacostello. He died, age 25, in Nov. 1905. Bridget was the daughter of Michael Ganley and Mary Conboy of Shanvaghera.

Mary Anne Freeman & Michael Carne
m. Feb. 1905 (Thomas Duffy & Bridget Freeman)

Note: Mary Anne was the daughter of Thomas Freeman of Ballinacostello.
Michael was the son of John Carne of Woodfield.

Thomas Freeman & Mary Glynn
m. March 1905 (Michael Freeman & Mary Finn)

Note: Thomas was the son of John Freeman of Esker. Mary was the daughter
of Thomas Glynn of Meeltran.

Mary Freeman & James Kelly
m. March 1905 (John Murtagh & Anne Boyle)

Note: Mary was the daughter of William Freeman of Ballinacostello. James
was the son of Patrick Kelly of Derrygay.

Timothy Freeman & Mary Anne Loghan
m. March 1909 (John Gavin & Mary Lyons)

Note: Timothy was the son of Thomas Freeman of Ballinacostello. Mary
Anne was the daughter of John Loghan of Tubber.

Anthony Freeman & Ellen Freeman
m. March 1912 (Anthony Cunnane & Kate Cunnane)

Note: Anthony was the son of Simon Freeman & Anne Caulfield of Carton
North.
Ellen was the daughter of Michael Freeman & Ellen Kane of Rath.

Bridget Ganley (nee Freeman) & William Lyons
m. Apr. 1912 (William Murphy & Maggie Lyons), Knock Parish

Note: Bridget, age 33, widow of Thomas Francis Freeman, was the daughter
of Michael Ganley and Mary Conboy of Shanvaghera. William, age 41, a
widower, was the son of Edward Lyons of Lismeegaun.

Bridget Freeman & Michael O'Connolly
m. July 1913 (Pat O'Boyle & Anne Snee)

Note: Bridget was the daughter of Timothy Freeman & Mary Bones of Derrycashel. Michael was the son of Michael O'Connolly of Castlerea.

Nora Freeman & Bernard Maguire
m. August 1920 (Peter Fleming & Winifred Nolan)

Note: Nora was the daughter of Michael Freeman & Mary Tarpey of Aghataharn. Bernard, age 31, was the son of John Maguire of Gurteen, Cloonfad, Co. Roscommon?

# Allen Families in the Vicinity of Ballybunion, County Kerry, in the 19<sup>th</sup> Century

There are two sources for the surname Allen in Ireland. The first source directly derives from the English or Scottish. The Scottish version originates as Mac Allion (translated as "rock"), a branch of the Campbell clan. The second source is an Anglicized version of the Irish *Hallion* or *O hAillion* (translated as "descendent of Ailion"). The Allen surname is uncommon along the West Coast of Ireland. It is more common in the East, specifically in Northern Ireland.

Penders 1659 Census

Edward Allen – "Ballyeghna & Ballynonane" in Killehenny Parish

Tithe Applotment Books

Denis Allen, Urlee East, Lisselton Parish (1823)

49

Edward Allen, Tarbert, Kilnaughtin Parish (1831)

Edward Allen, Tieraclea Lower, Kilnaughtin Parish (1831)

George Allen, Tarmon Hill, Kilnaughtin Parish (1831)

George Allen, Doonard Upper, Kilnaughtin Parish (1831)

House Tenure Books, 1850 (lessors in parentheses)

John Allen, Letter (Geo. Wren)
Margaret Allen, Ballyloughran (Denis Shea)
Michael Allen, Ballydonohoe (John Kinneally)
Michael Allen, Lahesheragh North (Patrick Francis)
Patrick Allen, Affouley (James Quinlan)
Patrick Allen, Inch East (James Quinlan)
Richard Allen, Doonard Lower, Tarbert (Mr. Leslie)
Richard Allen, Doonard Lower (John Mort)
Timothy Allen, Ballydonohoe (Timothy Kinneally)
Timy Allen, Tullamore (Maurice & John Griffin)

Griffith's Valuation – 1851

Catherine Allen, Affouley, Galey Parish

Denis Allen, Lahesheragh, Lisselton Parish

Johanna Allen, Letter, Aghavallen Parish

Patrick Allen, Tullamore, Kilconly Parish

Richard Allen, Tarbert, Kilnaughtin Parish (Bridewell St.)

Note: Richard Allen is described as a "baker" on Chapel St., Tarbert, in Slater's 1846 Directory.

<u>Listowel, Ballybunion & Ballylongford Parish Registers, Baptisms &</u>
<u>Marriages</u>

Catherine Allen & Thomas Meany
Lucy, Oct. 1808 (David Allen & Mary Connor), Listowel Parish

David Allen & Mary Connor
Mary, Dec. 1809 (Matthew Connelly), Gortcren?, Listowel
Lucy, Dec. 1811 (Charles Callaghan & Anne Barry)
Catherine, March 1817 (Honora Connor), Islandganiv
Michael, Sept. 1818 (Michael Hart & Honora Flahavin), Greenville
Ellen, Apr. 1820 (Patrick Kenny & Mary Carmody)
Catherine, March 1821 (Edward Connor & Bridget Connor)
Mark, Sept. 1827 (Richard Ryan & Mary Paltent), Listowel

Catherine Allen & James Dillon
Michael, Nov. 1810 (William Regan & Catherine Huson), Listowel Parish

Timothy Allen & Mary Gallivan
Michael, June 1831 (J. Moore & M. Dillane) Shrone, Listowel
John, July 1833 (Patrick Allen & Juliana Connor), Tullamore, Kilconly
Dermot, May 1835 (Patrick Ferris & Catherine Gallivan)
Bridget, Jan. 1838 (Bridget Gallivan)

Joanna (or Juliana) Allen & Thomas Stack
m. March 1832 (Robert Stack & Ed. Stack), Urlee
Mary, July 1835 (Michael Allen & Mary Colbert), Kilmulhane

John Allen & Margaret Molyneaux
George, May 1832 (J. Molyneaux & Elizabeth Stokes), Skehanierin, Listowel
Ann, May 1834 (Joanna Kennelly & Wm. Hopkins), Coolnanunagh?,
Ballylongford
Thomas, Jan. 1836 (William Molyneaux)
Margaret, Jan. 1838 (T. Molyneaux & E. Shanahan)
John, May 1842 (Thomas Molyneaux & Catherine O'Donnell), Carhunakilla?,
Ballylong.
Michael, Nov. 1844 (Andrew Molyneaux & Mary Culhane)

Ellen Allen & Thomas Francis
Joanna, Oct. 1832 (Michael Flahavin & Honora Grady), Glouria
Patrick, Jan. 1836 (Timothy O'Brien & Mary Mulvihill)
Margaret, July 1841 (Michael Allen & Margaret Carmody)
Thomas, Nov. 1842 (Catherine Francis)

Mary Allen & William Shanahan
Joanna, Oct. 1832 (James Francis & Mary Shanahan), Lahesheragh

Patrick Allen & Catherine Foley
Janet, Jan. 1833 (Dermot Sullivan & Mary Connor), Doon
William, Apr., 1838 (Michael Flahavin & Catherine Allen), Ahimma
Denis, Sept. 1841 (Patrick Nolan & Catherine Quinlan), Ahovola?
Mary, July 1844 (Patrick Connor & Michael Callaghan)

Catherine Allen & Michael Flahavin
m. June 1833 (Patrick Allen & Bridget Connell), Tullamore

Patrick Allen & Mary Fitzmaurice
Mary, Augt. 1833 (Patrick Murphy & Bridget Flahavin), Tullamore

Cornelius Allen & Margaret Dee
Martha, Sept. 1833 (Catherine Dee), Ballyloughran
Cleopatra, Dec. 1836 (Ellen Allen)

John Allen & Joanna Fealy
m. Apr. 1834 (Patrick Allen & James Farrell), Letter

Michael Allen & Mary Purtill
Liam, Augt. 1835 (Hanora Sullivan), Ballydonohoe
Monica, March 1840 (Ellen Sullivan)
Patrick, May 1842 (Hanora Purtill)
John, Augt. 1847 (Julia Connell), Farranastack

Patrick Allen & Joanna (or Hanora) Lynch
Margaret, Jan. 1836 (Henry Allen & Mary Allen), Tullamore
Patrick, Jan. 1838 (John Lynch & Honora Flahive)
Bridget, Apr. 1840 (Catherine Perriman)

Joanna Allen & Thomas Burke (Bourke)
m. Sept. 1838 (John Walsh & Mary Regan), Kilmulhane
Catherine, Oct. 1852 (Denis Allen & Catherine Shanahan), Barnadarrig

Cornelius Allen & Honora Barrett
m. Feb. 1841 (Margaret Barrett & Mary Scanlan), Gortnaskela
Henry, Dec. 1841 (Julia Reilly), Barracks
Mary, June 1850 (John Scanlan & Mary Scanlan), Gortnaskela
Mary, March 1855 (Michael Barrett & Ellen Barrett)
Michael, May 1858 (Patrick & Ellen Barrett), Lisselton
John, Oct. 1864 (Thomas Harty & Joanna Harty), Gortnaskela

Cornelius Allen & Margaret Dee
m. May 1841 (Roger Harty & Mary Hands), Ballyeagh [record of marriage verified]

Michael Allen & Margaret Deady (Dady)
m. July 1841 (Honora O'Brien & Margaret Savage), Killomeerhoe
John, Dec. 1844 (Michael Allen & Hanna Allen)
Michael, Nov. 1847 (Simon Mahoney & Ann Leonard)
Honora, Augt. 1850 (Timothy Coleman & Ellen Allen)

Ellen Allen & John Walsh
m. Feb.1842 (James Hartnett, Maurice Callaghan, Alex Moriarty), Killehenny

Margaret Allen & John Keefe
m. Feb. 1844 (Denis Lynch & Margaret Sweeney), Ballyconry

Elizabeth Allen & William Fealy (of Duagh Parish)
m. Feb. 1845 (Thomas Burke & Michael Allen), Lahesheragh

Mary Allen & John Callaghan
m. Feb. 1846 (John Lynch & John Flaherty), Lahesheragh
Thomas, Nov. 1847 (Denis & Johanna Allen), Lahardane
Anne, Apr. 1858 (Patrick & Mary Kennelly)

Denis Allen & Deborah Gallivan
m. Feb. 1851 (Maria Moriarty & Maria Gallivan), Lahesheragh

Michael, Sept. 1852 (Michael Allen & Elizabeth Allen)
Mary, June 1855 (James Gallivan & Catherine Enright)
Mary, Dec. 1857 (John Hannon & Ellen Hannon), Gale
Patrick, Feb. 1859 (Denis Gallivan & Honoria Murphy)
Margaret, July 1864 (Michl. Hannon & Mary Hannon; Michael Allen, brother, informant,)
James, Feb. 1867 (Thomas Callaghan; Michael Allen, informant)
Thomas, March 1871 (Catherine Hannon; Patrick Allen, informant)

Michael Allen & Hanora Barrett
Catherine, March 1852 (Michael Lane & Mary Lane), Scrahan?

Note: reference to Cornelius Allen & Honora Barrett above.

Patrick Allen & Elizabeth Harrington
m. July 1852 (James Walsh & Bridget Harrington)
Mary, Apr. 1856 (Henry Allen & Julia Lawlor)
Patrick, Feb. 1859 (John Allen & Hanora Allen), Killehenny
Timothy, 1862? [record requires verification]
Henry, Augt. 1864 (Thomas Purtill & Hanora Griffin), Trippul
Matthew, May 1867 (Michael Gorman & Joanna Gorman)
Bridget, Apr. 1870 (Patrick Gorman & Joanna Gorman)
Denis, Jan. 1873 (Patrick Sheehy & Mary Sheehy)

Michael Allen & Mary Sullivan
Denis, Jan. 1855 (Denis Allen & Joanna Allen)
Catherine, June 1856 (Martin Sullivan & Bridget Sullivan), Lahardane
Margaret, March 1857 (John Callaghan & Mary Allen)
James, June 1858 (John Mulvihill &? Sullivan), Ballyconry

Michael Allen & Mary Griffin
m. Feb. 1855 (William Ahern & James Walsh), Ahovola?
Catherine, Dec. 1855 (Denis Allen & Mary Allen), Aphola?
Bridget, 1858 (Honora White), Ahovola

John Allen & Elizabeth Sweeney
Anne, Jan. 1858 (Mary Moriarty), Lisselton
Margaret, Nov. 1859 (Timothy Mangan & Margaret Sweeney)

Henry, May 1862 (Patrick Sweeney & Honora Mangan)
Patrick, March 1865 (Michael Connell & Catherine Mangan), Moneen
Mary, March 1868 (Honora Perryman), Moybella
Honoria, June 1870 (civil record), Ballyegan
John, Dec. 1872 (Mary Buckley)

Note: John Allen was the son of John & Anne Allen. According to their granddaughter, Anne Carmody, Anne married Denis Reidy, Margaret married a man named Barry, Patrick married in Canada, Mary became a nun, Sister Hubert, in Canada, and John emigrated to Waterbury, CT. Henry married Mary Deenihan. Honoria married John Carmody.

John Allen & Johanna Linnane
Ellen, Jan. 1858 (Ellen Linnane), Gale
Timothy, c.1860 (no baptism record found)
John, c.1862 (no baptism record found)
Mary, Nov. 1865 (John Walsh & Ellen Walsh), Trippul
Henry, May 1868 (Martin Kennelly & Anne Mahoney)
Patrick, March 1871 (Mary Walsh)
Johanna, Apr. 1874 (Mary Costelloe)

Note: John Allen was the son of Timothy Allen & Mary Gallivan of Tullamore. Johanna Linnane was the daughter of Timothy Linnane & Ellen Keefe of Lacka. With the exception of Timothy, their children immigrated to Hoboken, New Jersey. Ellen married Denis Griffin in Apr. 1885. Timothy married Johanna Purtill in Feb. 1885. Mary married Patrick Lovett in Hoboken in July 1895. Henry married Margaret Campen in Hoboken in Apr. 1896. Patrick married Mary Ferris in Hoboken in Apr. 1906. Johanna married John Keane in Hoboken in Jan. 1902.

Honoria Allen & Eugene Neil
m. Augt. 1861 (Thomas Carey & Eugene O'Neil), Pullogh?, Listowel
Michael, May 1862 (Matthew Moloney & Mary Allen)
Patrick, March 1864 (Patrick Allen & Honora Connor), Listowel

Bridget Allen & William Linnane
m. Feb. 1863 (Patrick Ferris & Robert Cahill), Curraghderrig, Aghavallen
Patrick, Apr. 1868 (civil record)

Johanna, March 1870 (Thomas Flahive & Catherine O'Connor)
Mary, Jan. 1873 (James Moran & Catherine Connor), Glanawillin
Honora, June 1875 (John Coughlan & Julia Collins)

Michael Allen & Catherine Long
m. Nov. 1868 (Thomas Callaghan & Michael Allen), Lahesheragh

Note: Michael, a widower, was the son of Denis Allen of Lahesheragh. Catherine was the daughter of Jeremiah Long of Trippul.

Michael Allen & Mary Gallivan
Patrick, Apr. 1870 (Michael Gallivan & Johanna Allen), the Square, Listowel

Henry Allen & Mary Sullivan
m. Feb. 1871 (John Walsh & John Stack)
Patrick, March 1873 (Patrick Allen & Mary Allen), Ballyeagh

Note: Henry was the son of Cornelius Allen of Ballyeagh. Mary was the daughter of Dermit Sullivan & Juliana Kennelly of Ballydonohoe.

Patrick Allen & Catherine Granville
m. Jan. 1875 (John Nolan & Gerald Fleming), Listowel
Michael, Nov. 1875 (Patrick Murphy & Catherine Kennelly), Convent St., Listowel
Patrick, March 1878 (John Reilly & Johanna Murphy)

Note: Patrick, age 27, was the son of Michael Allen of Listowel. Margaret may be the daughter of Maurice Granville, dec'd., & Margaret Murphy of Listowel, born 1851.

Johanna Allen & Patrick Murphy
m. Nov. 1875 (Jeremiah Fitzgerald & Catherine Murphy), Listowel

Note: Joanna, age 19, was the daughter of Michael Allen of Listowel. Patrick, age 22, was the son of Patrick Murphy of Listowel.

Margaret Allen & Patrick Sullivan
m. Feb. 1876 (James Walsh & Johanna Sullivan), Beale

Martin, Nov. 1878 (Patrick Sullivan & Margaret Allen)
Honora, Augt. 1886 (Janet Linnane)

Note: Margaret was the daughter of Patrick Allen of Tullamore. Patrick was the son of Patrick Sullivan of Beale.

Mary Allen & John Linnane
m. Feb. 1876 (Edmund Kissane & Margaret Kissane)
Hanora, Feb. 1877 (Bridget Callaghan; Catherine Casey, informant), Killomeerhoe
Patrick, May 1882 (Bridget Callaghan)
John, Nov. 1884 (Thomas Allen & Deborah Gallivan)
Denis, Jan. 1887 (Ellen Healy)
James, June 1890 (John Cahill & Joanna Cahill)
Mary, June 1892 (Joanna Enright)

Note: Mary was the daughter of Denis Allen of Lahesheragh. John was the son of John Linnane of Lacka.

Mary Allen & David Dore
m. Feb. 1877 (Patrick Allen & Leanlan?), Ballyeagh
Joanna, Feb. 1879 (Mary Sullivan)
Patrick, Feb. 1883 (Margaret Stack)
Ellen, March 1885 (Joanna Scanlan), Barracks
Catherine, Nov. 1886 (Ellen Flaherty)
Cornelius, Oct. 1888 (Johanna Connor)
Margaret, Sept. 1890 (Margaret Scanlan), Ballyeagh
John, May 1892 (Bridget Deenihan)
David Patrick, May 1896 (Mary Flaherty)

Note: Mary was the daughter of Cornelius Allen of Ballyeagh. David was the son of Cornelius Dore & Johanna Stack of Ballyeagh. He was baptized in June 1853.

Patrick Allen & Margaret Beazley
m. Feb. 1881 (Michael Beazley & William Sullivan)
Hanora, Jan. 1882 (Mary Allen)
Mary, Augt. 1883 (Mary O'Connor)

Margaret, Sept. 1886 (Bridget Houlihan), Ballybunion
Catherine, Augt. 1888 (Mary O'Connor)

Note: Patrick was the son of Cornelius Allen of Ballyeagh. Margaret was the daughter of Robert Beazley of Ballybunion.

Anne Allen & Denis Reidy
m. July 1882 (James Fenaghty & Ellen Fenaghty)
Timothy, June 1882 (Honora Fitzgerald), Ballyegan
Joanna & Mary, May 1884 (Mary Griffin; Mary Fitzgerald)
John, August 1886 (Mary Allen)
Thomas, June 1888 (Honora Allen)
Elizabeth, Jan. 1891 (Honora Allen)
Denis, July 1893 (Honora Sweeney)
Patrick, Feb. 1897 (Mary Sweeney)
Henry, Sept. 1898 (Honora Sweeney)

Note: Anne was the daughter of John Allen & Elizabeth Sweeney of Ballyegan. Denis was the son of Timothy (Thad) Reidy & Johanna Mulvihill of Ballydonohoe. He was baptized in October 1856.

Mary Allen & Daniel Lyons
m. Feb. 1884 (Timothy Allen & Mary Sheehy)

Note: Mary was the daughter of Patrick Allen of Tullamore. Daniel was the son of Patrick Lyons of Shreelane?

Timothy Allen & Johanna Purtill
m. Feb. 1885 (Bartl. Flahive & Mary Flahive)
Thomas, March 1886 (Elizabeth Mulvihill), Ballybunion
Mary Teresa, Oct. 1887 (Janet Hanrahan)
Timothy, Feb. 1889 (civil record; Lizzie Purtill informant)
John Joseph, July 1890 (Catherine Purtill)
Elizabeth, Dec. 1891 (Mary Stack)
Joanna, June 1893 (Mary Walsh), Gortnaskela
Catherine, Feb. 1896 (Patrick Hayes & Elizabeth Purtill), Listowel
Christina, June 1897 (Thomas Allen & Elizabeth Purtill)
Patrick John, June 1901 (Michael Kirby & Teresa Dee)

Francis, Jan. 1903 (Patrick Allen & Catherine Purtill)
Gerard, Augt. 1906 (civil record)

Note: Timothy Allen was the son of John Allen & Johanna Linnane of Trippul. Johanna was the daughter of Thomas Purtill of Ballybunion & Elizabeth Gallivan of Lixnaw.

Ellen Allen & Denis Griffin
m. Apr. 1885 (John Allen & Michael Hanrahan)
Catherine, July 1886 (Johanna Allen), Trippul
John, Apr. 1888 (Johanna Allen)
Mary, March 1891 (civil record)
Hanora, June 1892 (Honora Hannafin)
Johanna, Jan. 1895 (civil record)
Johanna, Augt. 1897 (Bridget Callahan)
Ellen, Oct. 1901 (John Scanlan & Anne Scanlan)

Note: Ellen was the daughter of John Allen & Johanna Linnane of Trippul. Denis was the son of Martin Griffin & Catherine Connell of Ballyegan. After Denis died, Ellen and her children immigrated to Hoboken, New Jersey. The first Johanna died in 1896. Catherine married Patrick Ford in Hoboken in Apr. 1913. Mary married Patrick McNamara in New York in July 1917. Hanora married Michael Connor in New York in June 1921. Johanna married Charles Banda in New York in Nov. 1932. Ellen married Jerome Kleinicke in New York in 1931.

Henry Allen & Mary Deenihan
m. Sept. 1889 (Timothy Allen & Elizabeth Purtill)
Elizabeth, May 1891 (Catherine Brennan), Lacka
Mary Anne, Augt. 1892 (civil record)
Bridget, June 1895 (Catherine Deenihan), Farranastack
Anne, July 1897 (Mary Deenihan)
John, Nov. 1900 (Michael Griffin & Bridget Griffin)

Note: Henry was the son of John Allen & Elizabeth Sweeney of Ballyegan. Mary was the daughter of Martin Deenihan & Mary Fitzgerald of Ballybunion. She was baptized in June 1868.

Hanora Allen & John Carmody
m. Feb. 1891 (Patrick Barry & Mary Barry)
James, Apr. 1892 (Honora Deenihan), Ballyegan
Elizabeth, Oct. 1893 (Mary Connor)
Catherine, Oct. 1894 (Honora Sweeney)
John, Feb. 1897 (Bridget Sweeney)
Mary, Apr. 1899 (Mary Kennelly)
Anne, March 1901 (Mary Reidy)
Michael, May 1902 (civil record)
Hanoria, Sept. 1904 (civil record)
Margaret, Jan. 1907 (civil record)
Margaret, May 1909 (civil record)

Note: Hanora was the daughter of John Allen & Elizabeth Sweeney of Ballyegan. John may be the son of James Carmody & Catherine Murphy of Ballylongford. John was described as a "carpenter" in the civil records. James died in Oct. 1918. Hanoria died Apr. 1924. Margaret died in May 1909. According to Anne Carmody, John died in 1927, Hanora in 1958 [records require verification]. Anne Carmody immigrated to Philadelphia.

Thomas Allen & Mary Walsh
m. Feb. 1896 (John Barry & John Walsh)
Denis, March 1897 (John Walsh & Joanna Walsh), Lahesheragh
Elizabeth, Nov. 1898 (Denis Healy & Maggie Harmon)

Note: Thomas was the son of Denis Allen of Lahesheragh. Mary was the daughter of John Walsh & Elizabeth Hannon of Barnadarrig. Her baptism date was June 1874.

Bridget Allen & Michael Murphy
m. Feb. 1902 (William Driscoll & Martin Scanlan)

Note: Bridget was the daughter of Patrick Allen of Tullamore. Michael was the son of Edward Murphy of Lahardane.

Patrick Allen & Bridget Roche
m. Oct. 1906 (David Allen & John Roche), Listowel

Note: Patrick was the son of Patrick Allen & Catherine Granville. Bridget was the daughter of James Roche & Margaret Fenaghty of Listowel. Her baptism date was Sept. 1877, townland of Moybella.

Timothy Allen & Bridget Callaghan
m. July 1909 (Maurice Fitzmaurice & Katie Keefe)

Note: Timothy was the son of Timothy Allen & Elizabeth Purtil of Ballybunion. Bridget was the daughter of Maurice Callaghan & Bridget Ferris of Ballybunion. Her baptism date was June 1885, townland of Lahesheragh.

Thomas Allen & Mary Teresa Halpin
m. Feb. 1914 (Joseph Allen & Hannah Halpin)

Note: Thomas was the son of Timothy Allen & Johanna Purtill of Ballybunion. Mary Teresa was the daughter of John Halpin & Mary Connor of Ballybunion. Her baptism date was Oct. 1879 in Finuge.

Elizabeth Allen & James Moran
m. Jan. 1917 (Thomas Callaghan & Mary Allen)

Note: Elizabeth was the son of Henry Allen of Ballingowan. James was the son of Cornelius Moran & Catherine Lynch of Lahesheragh. His baptism date was Oct. 1881.

Catherine Allen & Patrick Devereaux
m. Dec. 1918 (Thomas Grogan & Maggie Devereaux)

Note: Catherine, described as a "cook," was the daughter of Patrick Allen of Ballybunion. Patrick, described as a "soldier," was the son of John Devereaux & Ellen Heffernan of Ballygrennan, Listowel?.

Anne Allen & Richard Deenihan
m. Jan. 1920 (John Dee & Mary Allen)

Note: Anne was the daughter of Henry Allen of Ballingowan. Richard was the son of Patrick Deenihan & Catherine Hayes of Ballydonohoe. His baptism date was May 1892, townland of Urlee.

Civil record of deaths (townlands and informants are in parentheses)

Mary Allen, Jan. 1868, 52, (Lahesheragh, Michael Allen)
Ellen Allen, Nov. 1870, 100, (Listowel workhouse)
Anne Allen, Oct. 1871, 76, widow, (Ballyegan, John Allen)
Mary Allen, Oct. 1872, 80, single nurse, (Beale, Thomas Carmody)
Honoria Allen, 1873, 40, single, (Lahardane, James Enright)
Timothy Allen, March 1873, 11, (Trippul, Patrick Allen)
Matthew Allen, March 1873, 5, (Trippul, Patrick Allen)
Johanna Allen, May 1873, 86, widow, (Rahavanig or Letter, William Linnane)
Mary Allen, March 1875, 58, married, (Convent St., Listowel, Johanna Allen)
Elizabeth Allen, Augt. 1875, 40, in childbirth, (Ballyegan, Michael Sweeney)
Michael Allen, Oct. 1890, 70, (Lahesheragh, Catherine Allen, wife)
Mary Allen, Jan. 1892, 9, (Listowel, Patrick Allen)
John Allen, May 1892, 70, widower, (Ballyegan, Honora Carmody)
Margaret Allen, Dec. 1893, 2, (Listowel, Patrick Allen)
Johanna Allen, March 1896, 59, (Trippul, John Allen, husband)
Bridget Allen, Apr. 1896, 10 mos., (Farranastack, Henry Allen)
Catherine Allen, May 1898, 80, widow, (Urlee, Listowel workhouse)
Denis Allen, Apr. 1899, 2, (Lahesheragh, Thomas Allen)
Cornelius Allen, Apr. 1903, 102, married, (Ballyeagh, David Dore)
Henry Allen, Oct. 1904, 58, single, (Ballyeagh, Mary Allen, sister)
Mary Allen, Dec. 1904, 85, widow, (Tarbert, Anne Ahern, niece)
Nora Allen, March 1905, 84, widow, (Ballyeagh, Kate Dore)
Patrick Allen, Apr. 1907, 60, married, (Listowel, Curraghatoosane hospital)
Elizabeth Allen, Jan. 1908, 75, widow, (Tullamore, Curraghatoosane hospital)
Denis Allen, Augt. 1908, 80, widower, (Lahardane, Curraghatoosane hospital)
Henry Allen, Jan. 1912, 45, married, (Hoboken, New Jersey)
John Allen, Dec. 1912, 79, widower, (Trippul, Curraghatoosane hospital)
Deborah Allen, Dec. 1915, 84, widow, (Lahesheragh, Deborah Allen, granddaughter)
Ellen Griffin (nee Allen), Sept. 1919, 61, widow, (New York, New York)
Mary Allen, Apr. 1924, 48, (Lahesheragh, Thomas Allen, husband)
John Allen, Jan. 1931, 70, single, (Hoboken, New Jersey)
Patrick Allen, July 1932, 73, married, (Ballybunion, Catherine Devereaux, daughter)
Margaret Allen, Augt. 1934, 76, widow, (Ballybunion, Catherine Devereaux, daughter)

Mary Allen, Sept. 1935, 8, (Tullamore, Julia Allen, mother)
Catherine Allen, Jan. 1937, 78, widow, (Listowel, John Allen, son)
Johanna Keane (nee Allen), Oct. 1939, 65, married, (Hoboken, New Jersey)
Timothy Allen, July, 1940, 77, married, (Ballybunion, John Allen, son)
Patrick Allen, June, 1941, 62, married, (Listowel, Margaret Allen, daughter)
Henry Allen, June 1945, 79, married, (Ballingowan, John Allen, son)
Joseph Allen, Augt. 1945, 2 days, (Ballybunion, Eamon Allen)
Mary Allen, Oct. 1945, 76, widow, (Ballingowan, Mary O'Carroll, daughter)
Thomas Allen, Oct. 1945, 72, married, (Lahesheragh, Dora Allen, daughter)
Mary Lovett (nee Allen), Sept. 1949, 84, widow, (Hoboken, New Jersey)
Patrick Allen, Nov. 1952, 81, married, (Teaneck, New Jersey)

St. John's Cemetery, Ballybunion

Cecie Lovett, 12 Nov. 1963
Her mother, Mary Allen, 22 Dec. 1963
Tom Allen, 6 Oct. 1967

Patrick Allen, Lahesheragh, 4 Feb. 1972
Catherine, his wife, 3 March 1993

Maura Lynch (nee Allen), Doon East, 24 Jan. 1985

Joseph Stephen Allen, 6 Sept. 1986

Liam Allen, "Sun Cottage", Sandhill Rd., 26 Jan. 1992

"In loving memory of our dear parents, Patrick Allen, Sandhill Rd., Ballybunion, d. 87 years, 15 June 1989, his loving wife Kathleen (nee McCarthy), d. 30 Jan. 1990, age 88"

Killehenny Cemetery

Timothy Allen, 4 Dec. 1959, age 70, his wife, Bridget (nee O'Callaghan), 30 March 1970, their son Eammon, d. 15 March 1986

Henry Allen, Ballyeagh, 27 July 1990, age 63

Mary Allen, Lahesheragh, d. 8 Apr. 1924, her husband, Thomas, d. 28 March 1945, Dora, Oct. 1988, age 85, her mother, Deborah, died 1915

Allen Records in Tarbert (Kilnaughtin Parish)

Edmund Allen & Catherine Hudson
m. May 1786 (no other details)
Eleanor, Apr. 1798 (no other details)
Mary Anne, May 1801 (no other details)
Edmund, Jan. 1806 (no other details)

Patrick Allen
burial, May 1796

John Allen, baptized Feb. 1797 (no other details)

George Allen & Eleanor Allen
Patrick, May 1797 (no other details)

Ellen Allen
burial, 1809

Mary Allen & William Murray
m. Jan. 1811 (James Murray & Jane Smith)

Catherine Allen & James?
m. Apr. 1825

Note: James is described as a soldier in His Majesty's 25th Regiment.

George Allen & Mary Teskey
m. Augt. 1826 (no other details)

Note: occupation given as "policeman."

Catherine Allen
burial, June 1830

Mary Allen
baptized Oct. 1831 (no other details)

George Allen
burial, Dec. 1832

Mary Allen & Jeremiah Hegarty
m. Augt. 1832 (no other details)

Richard Allen & Mary Ahern
m. Feb. 1844 (William Ahern & Michael Lac)
Anne, Augt. 1846 (Maurice Cunneen & Francis Allen), Tarbert
Ellen, Dec. 1848 (Ellen Ahern & Michael Langan)

Anne Allen & Thomas Fitzgerald
m. July 1860 (James Sullivan & Michael Ahern)

Ellen Allen & James Duggan
m. July 1869 (Richard Allen & Michael Hinchy)

Note: Ellen was the daughter of Richard Allen, postmaster of Tarbert. James was the son of James Duggan of Tarbert Island.

Frances Allen & Michael O'Leary
m. Apr. 1874 (William Dreslin & James Duggan)

Note: Francis was the daughter of Richard Allen, dec'd., shopkeeper, Tarbert. Michael was the son of Michael O'Leary, dec'd. national schoolteacher, Tarbert.

Henry Allen & Ellen O'Connell
m. Jan. 1914 (Maurice O'Connell & Mary Downey)

Henry, described as "Coast Guard," was the son of George Allen of Tarbert Island. Ellen was the daughter of Donal O'Connell of Doonard, Tarbert.

*Dennis Ford*

<u>Boston *Pilot's* Missing Friends Column</u> (Boston newspaper, 4 July 1885)

"Of Mary Shanahan, daughter of William Shanahan & Mary Allen who lived in Urlee, Lisselton, Co. Kerry. She left home about 33 years ago, in company with Johanna Wolfe, daughter of Richard Wolfe of Ballybunion. When last heard of, she went to Illinois. Information will be thankfully received by Johanna Shanahan, Cuba, Alleghany Co., NY."

# Linnane Families in the Vicinity of Ballybunion in the 19ᵗʰ Century

The Linnane surname originates in the Irish *O Leannain*, meaning "descendent of lover" and in *O Lonain*, meaning "descendent of blackbird." There appear to be three places of origin—counties Galway, Mayo and Fermanagh. The Connacht origin is said to derive from a brother of Niall of the Nine Hostages.

The name was spelled in a variety of ways—Linnane, Linane, Lennane, Lenane, Lennon, Leonane, Lynane—so it's impossible to say whether these variations represent the same or different septs. (Records are not included for the surname Leyne, as this appears to be a different sept related to the English surname Lyons.) In the parish books the variations were written interchangeably and inconsistently. Both in Ireland and in America, the name was Anglicized in official documents as "Leonard." To further complicate the matter, there were families of the professional class named "Leonard" in the Listowel area. The name was written in an American census in the way it may have sounded—"Leynert."

Except in cases where the name was clearly "Leonard" or "Lynane," the name is standardized—rightly or wrongly—as "Linnane."

Pigot's Directory, 1824

John Leonard, hotel & wholesale grocer, Listowel

Church & Leonard, corn merchants & millers, Listowel

Tithe Applotment Books, 1825 - 1826

John Leonard, Ballybunion, Killehenny

John Leonard, Ballygowloge, Listowel

John Leonard, Clievragh, Listowel

John Leonard, Curraghatoosane, Listowel

John Leonard, Gortcurren, Listowel

John Leonard, Inch the Castle, Listowel

John Leonard, Killehenny, Killehenny Parish

John Leonard, Town Fields, Listowel

Linnane & Gallivan, Farranpierce, Killehenny

M. Lennane, Lacka East, Lisselton

Thomas Leonard, Inch the Castle, Listowel

William Lenane & Co., Gortagrane West,?

Slater's Directory, 1846

Miss Jane Leonard, gentry, the Square, Listowel

Maurice Lennard, attorney, the Square, Listowel

<u>Valuation Office, House & Tenure Books 1848 – 1852</u> (lessors in parentheses)

Daniel Leonard, Clievragh (Lord Listowel)
Daniel Leonard, Gortcurreen
Daniel Leonard, Listowel (Lord Listowel)
David Leonard, Gortacrossane (Lord Listowel)
Denis Leonard, Ballybunion
Edmond Leonard, Barnadarrig (Mrs. Church)
Honoria Leonard, Lacka East (Maurice Leonard)
James Leonard, Killehenny (Miss Locke)
James Leonard, Killehenny (Thomas Leonard)
Jno. Leonard, Ballybunion (Mrs. Harena)
John Leonard, Ballybunion (Mrs. Haring)
John Leonard, Gortacrossane (Daniel Leonard)
Joseph Leonard, Loughanes (Edward Stack)
Kate Leonard, Farranastack
Manelo Leonard, Ballygowloge (Lord Listowel)
Maurice Leonard, Derra (George Gun)
Maurice Leonard, Lacka East (George Raymond)
Maurice Leonard, Lacka East (Maurice Leonard)
Michael Leonard, Lacka East (David Kissane)
Michael Leonard, Lacka East (George Raymond)
Maurice Leonard, Ballygowloge (Lord Listowel)
Maurice Leonard, Listowel (Lord Listowel)
Ned Leonard, Barnadarrig (Mrs. Church)
Ned Leonard, Barnadarrig (S. Raymond)
Patrick Leonard, Ballydonohoe (Richard Connor)
Thomas Leonard, Barnadarrig (Mrs. Church)
Thomas Leonard, Killehenny (Miss Locke)
Thomas Leonard, Killomeerhoe (Jas. Boyle & Wm. Buckley)
Thomas Leonard, Lacka East (Maurice Leonard)
William Leonard, Farrenpierce (Thomas Stradford)
William Leonard, Lacka East (George Raymond)
William Leonard, Rahavanig (Mrs. Church)

Griffith's Valuation, 1852

Maurice Lennane, Derra, Galey Parish

Patrick Lennane, Ballydonohoe,

William Lennane, Rahavanig, Kilconly Parish

Edmond Leonard, Barnadarrig, Killehenny Parish
Thomas Leonard

Daniel Leonard, Clievragh, Lisselton Parish

Honoria Leonard, Lacka East
Maurice Leonard (William)
Michael Leonard (Michael)
Thomas Leonard
William Leonard

Joseph Leonard, Loughanes

Daniel Leonard, Gortacrossane, Listowel
John Leonard

Daniel Leonard, Listowel

Daniel Leonard, Esq., Listowel, the Square
Maurice Leonard, Esq.

Maurice Leonard, Esq., Ballygowloge

Listowel, Ballybunion & Ballylongford Parish Registers, Baptims & Marriages

Maurice Leonard & Elizabeth Leonard
Cornelius, Augt. 1806 (Thomas Stack & Ann Stack), Listowel Parish

Jane Linnane & Bartholomew Stack
Bridget, Jan. 1808 (Matthew Daly & Mary Daly), Clievragh

Mary, Apr. 1814 (James Moloney & Ellen Mansil)
James, Dec. 1815 (Dermot Scanlan & Ann Barry)
Sarah, May 1818 (Thomas Marshall & Mary Stack)

Note: the name is also given as "Leonard" and in two records the mother's name is given as "Ellen."

John Leonard & Mary Caraney
Mary, Feb. 1810 (Thomas Connor & Elizabeth Shea), Listowel Parish

? Leonard & Helen Shanahan
Catherine, Jan. 1811 (Maurice Dillon & Mary Lyne), Listowel Parish

John Leonard & Mary Tyther
Margaret, Nov. 1811 (John Tyther & Mary Keily), Listowel Parish

John Leonard & Catherine Cronin
John, Feb. 1813 (John Curtin & M. Curtin), Listowel Parish

Catherine Leonard & Martin Broder
Martin, Feb. 1817 (Gerald Gallivan & Honora Lyne), Skehanierin, Listowel
John, June 1818 (Maurice Connor & Mary Louny)

John Leonard & Ann Egan
Janet, May 1817 (Daniel Leonard & Mary Healy), Listowel Parish
Sarah, July 1819 (James Church & Mrs. Leonard)
Ellen, Feb. 1821 (William Galway & Mary Egan)
Cornelius, Feb. 1822 (Thomas Leonard & Elizabeth Egan)
Daniel, Apr. 1825 (John Healy & Winifred Calahan)
Sarah, Dec. 1826 (John McCarthy & Agnes Carroll)
Margaret, July 1828 (Daniel Egan)
William, July 1830 (Daniel Egan & Mary Egan)

Elizabeth Linnane & Gerald Gallivan
Bridget Augt. 1817 (Denis Kelleher & Catherine Linnane), Listowel Parish
Mary, Nov. 1822 (Michael Gallivan & Catherine Gray)
Catherine, Nov. 1827 (Dermot Naughton & Margaret Naughton), Church Lane, Listowel

Joanna, Apr. 1830 (Patrick Brown & Mary Hegarty)
John, July 1832 (P. Nachton & Johanna Stack)

Ellen Linnane & Timothy Scanlan
Mary, Sept. 1818 (Maurice Scanlan & Mary Scanlan), Leitrim, Listowel
Maurice, July 1823 (John Fitzgerald & Ellen Fitzgerald)
Timothy, Jan. 1826 (James Ahern & Margaret Scanlan)
Michael, Dec. 1829 (Patrick Mulvihill & Honora Scanlan)

Mary Leonard & Michael Collins
Ellen, July 1820 (M. Kiely & Mary Stack), Listowel Parish
John, July 1823 (Timothy Healy & Honora Courich)

Catherine Linnane & Denis Nowlan
Catherine, July 1825 (John Sullivan & Mary Linnane), Gortacrossane, Listowel
Timothy, Augt. 1828 (Oliver Dalton & Catherine Stack)

Timothy Linnane & Ellen Connor
Ellen, June 1827 (no sponsors listed), Tullahennel, Ballylongford
Mary, Sept. 1828 (Cornelius Lyne & Bridget Connor)
Thomas, Dec. 1836 (Richard Bunion & Mary Roche), Glannanish?

Jeremiah Linnane & Catherine Connor
Johanna, Sept. 1827 (John Linnane & Johanna Connor), Dromakee, Lixnaw
Parish

Ellen Lennane & Timothy Healy
Johanna, Nov. 1827 (Michael Kelly & Mary Kilmane?), Church Lane, Listowel

Mary Linnane & Michael McNamara
William, March 1830 (William Dooling & Johana Crowly), Behens?, Listowel
Parish
Thomas, Augt. 1832 (D. Murphy & J. McNamara)
John, Sept. 1837 (Timothy McAuliffe & Mary McAuliffe) Skehanierin
Bridget, Feb. 1843 (Thomas Leonard & Bridget Connor)

Note: the name was also given as "Leonard."

John Linnane & Mary Flaherty
Mary, May 1830 (Denis Moran & Catherine Flahavin), Gortacrossane
Ellen, Jan. 1833 (J. Flaherty & M. Reily)

Note: the name was also given as "Leonard."

Edmund Linnane & Ellen Mulvihill, Shrone, Listowel
Edmund, Jan. 1831 (M. Collins & M. Mulvihill)

Mary Lennane & Patrick Griffin
Patrick, Apr. 1832 (Maurice Griffin & Mary Mingane?), Ballyconry

Timothy Linnane & Mary Keefe
John, June 1832 (Mary Ruddle), Killomeerhoe
Thomas, Apr. 1836 (Catherine Sullivan)

Note: this may be the same family listed below as Timothy Linnane and Ellen Keefe.

Maurice Linnane & Margaret Kennelly
William, Jan. 1833 (James Hennessy & Mary Kennelly), Lacka
Maurice, Jan. 1840 (William Linnane & Mary Barry)
John, May 1847 (Patrick Kennelly & Catherine Kennelly)

Maurice Linnane & Margaret Farrell
William, June 1833 (Martin Collins & Margaret Leyne), Lacka

William Linnane & Mary Molyneaux
Mary, Nov. 1833 (John Molyneaux & Bridget Molyneaux), Killomeerhoe

John Linnane & Margaret Harty
m. May 1834 (Thomas Harty & Michael Harty), Lacka
Patrick, March 1840 (Margaret Corridon)
Mary, Jan. 1842 (Margaret Linnane)
Margaret, Sept. 1844 (Margaret Quilter)
Ellen, June 1847 (Margaret Harty)

Note: the name was also given as "Leonard."

Timothy Linnane & Mary Sullivan
m. Nov. 1834 (Roger Sullivan & Catherine Sullivan), Ballylongford Parish
Mary, Nov. 1835 (Roger Sullivan & Mary Sullivan)

Note: in Mary's baptism record, father's personal name is given as "Roger."

William Linnane & Mary Gallivan
Joanna, May 1834 (John Walsh & Anne Hayes), Farranpierce, Killehenny
Anne, May 1837 (William Walsh & Mary Callihan)
Maurice, Jan. 1844 (Michael Gallivan & Mary Gallivan)

Maurice Linnane & Catherine Linnane, Ballybunion Parish
Catherine, Dec. 1834 (no record of godparents)

Joanna Linnane & James Hennessey
Dermot, July 1835 (Dermot Hennessey), Lyre, Lisselton
Ellen, May 1837 (no sponsors given)
Michael, May 1839 (Michael Costello & Margaret Harty), Rahrou [Rathroe?]
Catherine, June 1842 (Mary Hennessy)
James, Oct. 1844 (William Linnane & Sara Linnane)

Cornelius Linnane & Janet King
m. Feb. 1836 (John King & Cornelius Farrell), Letter, Ballylongford
William, Jan. 1837 (John Linnane & Ann Murphy)

Maurice Linnane & Deborah Lynch
m. Feb. 1836 (John Lynch & Ed Shanahin) Doon, Killehenny Parish
Margaret, Augt. 1839 (Ellen Enright), Derra
William, June 1849 (James Walsh & Mary Connor)
Michael, May 1855 (John Kissane & Catherine Kissane)

Note: Deborah's name also written as "Gobenet."

Timothy Linnane & Ellen Keefe
Johanna,? [no record located]
Thomas, Sept. 1837 (no sponsers listed), Killomeerhoe
Mary, Feb. 1843 (Ellen Courtney), Lacka
Patrick, July 1845 (James Hennessy & Sara Linnane)

Note: Mary immigrated to Hoboken, NJ.

Margaret Linnane & Patrick Cain
m. Feb. 1838 (William Linnane & Maurice Linnane), Lacka
Dermot, July 1839 (Joanna Linnane), Keelarda?

Note: the surname "Cain" is also given as "Keane." This may be the same
family listed below as Mary Linnane & Patrick Keane.

Joseph Linnane & Frances Quilter
m. Feb. 1838 (John Linnane & Matthew Quilter), Ballydonohoe
John, June 1839 (Edward Stack & Juliana Mahony), Loughanes [Loughanes?]
William, Oct. 1845 (Francis Quilter & Arabella Stack)
Maurice, Apr. 1855 (Thomas Bunyan & Johanna Quilter)
Joseph, Oct. 1858 (John Stack & Catherine Stack), Lisselton

Bridget Linnane & Morgan Dooling
m. Feb. 1839 (Joseph Linnane & Edward Walsh), Killehenny Parish
Mary, June 1840 (Patrick Griffin & Margaret Wolfe)
Patrick, Dec. 1843 (Michael Collins & Ellen Collins)
Catherine, Jan. 1846 (James Linnane & Catherine Kissane)

Note: in Patrick's baptism record the family name was spelled "Dowling."

Thomas Leonard & Hanora Hickey
Fabian, Augt. 1839 (Ellen Broderick), Killomeerhoe

David Linnane & Ellen Ahern
William, May 1840 (Hanora Ahern), Kilgarvin, Galey
Timothy, Jan. 1846 (John Linnane & Joanna Linnane)

Maurice Linnane & Honora Foley (Foulou)
m. Feb. 1841 (William Linnane & Daniel Foley), Ballingowan, Lisselton
Michael, Nov. 1843 (Michael Linnane & Catherine Linnane)
Timothy, Feb. 1847 (Patrick Griffin & Mary Foley)
William, Sept. 1851 (Michael Linnane & Johanna Purcell)

Note: in William's baptism record, his mother's name was given as "Mary."

Thomas Linnane & Bridget Kennelly
Mary, Feb. 1842 (John Houlihan & Ellen Dillon), Killomeerhoe
William, Apr. 1844 (John Kennelly & Ann Kennelly)
Anastasia, July 1846 (Thomas Leonard & Patrick Ryan), Keelimeerauge?
Patrick, March 1858 (William Linnane & Mary Mulvihill), Lacka
Michael, Oct. 1861 (Michael McElligott & Catherine McElligott)
Timothy, July 1865 (John Linnane & Honora Lynch), Lacka

Note: given the long stretch of years, the records may reflect two families with the same surnames. The name was also given as Leonard.

John Linnane & Catherine Moloney
William, May 1842 (Mary Hefferon), Ballingowan
Mary, Sept. 1843 (Bridget Moloney)
John, Augt. 1845 (William Linnane & Mary Moloney)
Catherine, June 1847 (Bridget Moloney)
Patrick, Feb. 1849 (Mary Moloney)

Note: the name was also given as "Leonard."

Timothy Linnane &?? (no mother indicated), Ballylongford Parish
Helen, Nov. 1842 (John Bunion & Mary Bunion)

?? Linnane & Juliana Connor
Joanna, Nov. 1842 (Timothy Quilter & Margaret Quilter), Ballydonohoe

Catherine Linnane & Michael Fitzgerald
John, Jan. 1843 (William Linnane & Sara Linnane), Lacka

John Linnane & Mary Ferris
William, Feb. 1843 (James Ferris & Honora Ferris), Gortacrossane
Maurice, June 1852 (Patrick Ferris & Bridget Ferris)

Margaret Linnane & John Coghlan
Mary, Jan. 1844 (John Carmody & Ellen Marshall), Larha, Ballylongford
Joanna, Jan. 1846 (Maurice Linnane & Juliana Purcel) [record needs verification]
Denis, Apr. 1848 (no sponsors given)

Mary, Augt. 1850 (no sponsors given)
Patrick, Feb. 1853 (no sponsors given)
John, Nov. 1857 (John Delane & Mary Cahill)
Ellen, Apr. 1860 (Thomas Dillane & Johanna Fealy)
Margaret, Apr. 1862 (Ellen Carmody)

Note: in Denis's baptism record the father's name is given as "Daniel." Their daughter, Hanora, married Michael O'Connor, the son of Michael O'Connor and Catherine Healy of Larha, in Feb. 1890.

John Linnane & Margaret Kissane
m. Jan. 1845 (Michael Kissane & Maurice Lennane), Urlee
Michael, Feb. 1846 (Michael Kissane & Margaret Connell)
Joanna, May 1848 (David Kissane & Ellen Kissane), Lacka

Sara Linnane & Dermot Long
m. Feb. 1845 (William Linnane & Edmund Walsh)
Catherine, Apr. 1846 (Catherine Mullins), Lacka
Patrick, March 1854 (Patrick Long & Mary Sullivan)
Michael, Augt. 1859 (Bartholomew Long & Johanna Linnane)

Note: in the baptism records, the father's personal name was also given as "Jeremiah."

James Linnane & Honora Flaherty
m. May 1845 (Thomas Buckley & Edmund Hayes)
William, Feb. 1846 (William Linnane & Catherine Flaherty)

Note: James was from Castleisland. Honora was from Ballybunion.

John Linnane & Mary Enright
m. Feb. 1846 (Denis Enright & Patrick Scanlan), Farranpierce

Thomas Linnane & Johanna Scanlan
Mary, Dec. 1846 (Edmund Sage & Mary Scanlan)
Julia, Dec. 1846, Mary's twin (Edmund Savage & Anabella Scanlan), Gortnaskeha
Mary, Augt. 1848 (Edmund Leonane & Mary Walsh), Barnadarrig

John, Nov. 1850 (John Scanlan & Catherine Scanlan), Lahardane
Ellen, Oct. 1852 (John Scanlon & Johanna Scanlon)
Johanna, June 1859 (Timothy Buckley & Mary Buckley)

Note: the name was also given as "Leonard."

John Lynane & Bridget McMahon
m. Feb. 1847 (Edmund Fitzmaurice & Maurice Sweeny), Gale
Patrick, Apr. 1849 (Thomas McMahon & Catherine McMahon), Coolkeragh

Margaret Leonard & Francis Gentleman
Richard, May 1847 (James Gentleman), Ballylongford Parish
Margaret, Apr. 1848 (Susanna Crilly)
Francis, May 1850 (no sponsors indicated)
Mary Anne, Dec. 1851 (John Gentleman)
Ellen, Feb. 1853 (John Gentleman & Ellen Twyford)
Francis, March 1856 (Thomas Curtayne)

John Linnane & Joanna Hennessy
Margaret, June 1849 (Mary Gallivan), Lacka

Ellen Leonard & Denis Quilter
m. July 1849 (Edmund Leonard & Matthew Quilter), Barnadarrig

Maurice Leonard, Esq., & Jane Leonard
Mary, March 1849 (no sponsors given), Listowel
Catherine Jane, Augt. 1850 (no sponsors given)

Maurice Leonard & Mary Broder
Mary, Oct. 1851 (James Leonard & Mary Leonard), Listowel Parish
John, Oct. 1851, Mary's twin (Daniel Leonard & Mary Broder)

John Linnane & Mary Flahavin
m. Feb. 1853 (Patrick Connor & James Walsh) Lahardane
Mary, July 1853 (Michael Divane & Joanna Divane), Tullabeg

Patrick Leonard & Mary Trant
Maurice, Sept. 1853 (Maurice Trant & Mary Trant), Ennismore, Listowel

William Linnane & Johanna Quane?
m. Nov. 1853 (John Sullivan & Hanora Flahavin), Tullamore, Kilconly

William Linnane & Joanna Cooney
Mary, Nov. 1854 (John Stack & Joanna Divane), Gullane, Kilconly

William Linnane & Honora Coghlan
Maurice, Nov. 1855 (John King & Mary Elligott), Letter

Mary Linnane & Patrick Keane
John, March 1856 (John Keane & Mary Linnane), Gale
Catherine, March 1859 (John Lynch & Mary Lynch)
Margaret, [baptism record not found]

Note: Margaret married Edmund Connor of Greenville in Feb. 1874. Edmund
was the son of Thomas Connor & Catherine Hayes.

Bridget Linnane & Patrick Mulvihill
m. Feb. 1857 (Daniel Keane & James Murphy), Kilgarvan
Julia, Dec. 1857 (John Mulvihill & Julia Linnane)
Edmund, Feb. 1860 (Michael Lynch & Margaret Buckley)
Ellen, June 1864 (William Mulvihill & Catherine Linnane)
Michael, Apr. 1867 (John Buckley & Joanna Mulvihill)
Thomas, 1870 (Ellen Buckley)
Patrick, Feb. 1875 (Bridget Lynch)

Note: for Ellen's baptism, Catherine Lynch of Kilgarvan was described as
"aunt" in the civil record.

Patrick Linnane & Margaret Linnane
Michael, Augt. 1857 (Edmund Murphy & Johanna Sullivan), Killehenny
Parish

Johanna Linnane & John Allen
Ellen, Jan. 1858 (Ellen Linnane), Gale
Timothy, c. 1860 (no baptism record found)
John, c. 1862 (no baptism record found)
Mary, Nov. 1865 (John Walsh & Ellen Walsh) Trippul, Kilconly

Henry, May 1868 (Martin Kennelly & Anne Mahoney)
Patrick, March 1871 (Mary Walsh)
Johanna, Apr. 1874 (Mary Costelloe)

Note: John Allen was the son of Timothy Allen & Mary Gallivan of Tullamore. Johanna Linnane was the daughter of Timothy Linnane & Ellen Keefe of Lacka. With the exception of Timothy, their children immigrated to Hoboken, New Jersey. See the Allen chapter for marriage records of their children.

Daniel Linnane & Mary Mulvihill
Margaret, June 1858 (Richard Hayes & Mary Linnane), Ballybunion Parish

Bridget Linnane & Michael Houlihan
m. June 1858 (Jeremiah Lyne & Mary Barrett), Listowel Parish
Mary, March 1860 (James Keane & Mary Keane) Affouley, Galey
James, May 1862 (John Houlihan & Hanora Trant)
John, Dec. 1864 (William Murphy & Catherine Trant)
Hanora, May 1867 (Maurice Linnane & Hanora Trant)
Margaret, May 1875 (Honora Houlihan)
Catherine, Apr. 1878 (Joanna Buckley)
Michael, 1869 (John Houlihan & Margaret Murphy)
Thomas, Oct. 1880 (Honora Griffin)

Note: The name also appears as "Leonard." Michael Houlihan was from Ennismore.

Bridget Lynan & James Casey
m. Jan. 1860 (Patrick Lynan & Patrick Casey), Listowel
James, Nov. 1860 (Nicholas Synan & Margaret Synan), Shrone
Mary, March 1869 (Ellen Lynon), Dirrah, Listowel
James, March 1869, Mary's twin (Ellen Mulvihill)

Note: James Casey was from Shrone, Listowel. Bridget's surname is spelled "Synan" in the parish register.

Denis Lynan & Elizabeth Mangane
m. Jan. 1861 (Patrick Lyne & Patrick Dillon), Cloonmackon, Listowel
Patrick, July 1866 (civil record; name written as "Synan.")

James Linnane & Dorothy Quinn
Arthur, Feb. 1861 (Daniel Cuisidine? & Mary Crimmins), Listowel Parish
Vincent, March 1863 (Johanna Regan & Denis O'Brien), Woodford, Listowel

James Linnane & Mary Hughes
Daniel, July 1861 (Daniel Linnane & Ellen Cussen), Listowel Parish

John Linnane & Mary Lovett
m. July 1861 (John Lovett & Timothy Lyne), Glouria
Catherine, July 1862 (John Lovett & Ellen Keefe)
Timothy, June 1864 (Catherine Walsh)
John, May 1866 (John Lovett & Mary Linnane)
Ellen, Dec. 1868 (John Cox & Honora Cox)
Mary, Jan. 1871 (Catherine Lovett)
Thomas, Dec. 1872 (Honora Coughlan)
Joanna, Apr. 1875 (Joanna Linnane)
Patrick, Jan. 1878 (Joanna Linnane; Catherine Linnane present)

Note: Catherine married Michael Galvin in Sept. 1892. Ellen married
Thomas Carmody in Dec. 1890. Mary married Thomas McCarthy in June
1896. Patrick married Margaret Doody in Feb. 1900. The last three marriages
took place in Hoboken, New Jersey.

Mary Linnane & Florence? McCarthy
m. Jan. 1863 (Joseph McCarthy & Maurice Linnane), Lisselton

William Linnane & Bridget Allen
m. Feb. 1863 (Patrick Ferris & Robert Cahill), Curraghderrig, Ballylongford
Patrick, Apr. 1868 (civil record)
Johanna, March 1870 (Thomas Flavin & Catherine Connor)
Mary, Jan. 1873 (James Moran & Catherine Connor), Glanawillin
Honora, June 1875 (John Coghlan & Julia Collins)

James J. Leonard & Mary Anne Proctor
Mary, Feb. 1863 (Daniel Leonard & William Leonard), Listowel Parish
George, Apr. 1864 (Richard Cusson & Ann Cusson)

Note: James was described as a civil engineer.

Mary Linnane & Patrick Purcell
m. Feb. 1863 (Patrick Purcell & Ellen Breen), Lisselton Parish

Ellen Linnane & Richard O'Connor
Agnes, Jan. 1864 (John Dillane & Johanna Linnane), Listowel Parish

Mary Lynan & Darby Curnane
Mary, May 1864 (civil record), Garryard, Galey

Bridget Linnane & Robert Buckley
Robert, May 1864 (civil record), Duagh Parish

Patrick Lynane & Biddy Kinnelly
Michael, May 1865 (civil record, Mary Kinnelly, grandmother), Newton Sandes, Murher

Michael Linnane & Elizabeth Fitzgerald
m. Feb. 1866 (James Walsh & Johanna Kissane), Ballybunion Parish

Note: Michael was the son of William Linnane of Addergower? Elizabeth was the daughter of John Fitzgerald, dec'd., of Farranpierce.

William Linnane & Bridget Coleman
Cornelius, May 1866 (civil record) Kilcolman, Ballylongford

John Linnane & Johanna Roche
m. Jan. 1867 (James Carr & Richard Hayes), Kilgarvan
David, May 1868 (Thomas Scanlon & Bridget Scanlon)

Note: John was the son of David Linnane of Kilgarvin. Johanna was the daughter of Francis Roche of Kilgarvin.

Ellen Lynan & James Enright
m. Apr. 1867 (Maurice Wallace & Nicholas Lynan), Listowel Parish
John, Jan. 1869 (civil record), Derra

Note: Ellen, age 23, was the daughter of Edmond Lynan of Shrone, Listowel. (Her surname is listed as "Synon.") James, age 22, was the son of John Enright of Shrone.

Joanna Linnane & James Beasley
m. Feb. 1868 (Edmund Carey & Patrick Linnane), Lixnaw Parish
Michael, Nov. 1868 (Mary Carmody)
Mary, Jan. 1870 (Michael Beasley & Margaret Beasley)
Johanna, March 1871 (Timothy Relihan & Mary Relihan)
Julia, July 1872 (Thomas Linnane & Margaret Connor)
Maurice, Nov. 1873 (Ann Carroll)
Daniel, Feb. 1875 (Patrick Reidy & Mary Reidy)
Margaret, Augt. 1876 (Johanna Donoghue)
Patrick, Jan. 1878 (Daniel Relihan & Elizabeth Relihan)
Hanora, May 1879 (Johanna Connor)
James, Dec. 1882 (Michael Relihan & Mary Lyons)
Ellen, May 1884 (James Lacy & Mary Carroll)
Sara, Sept. 1886 (Maurice Beasley & Julia Beasley)

Note: Joanna, age 24, was the daughter of Patrick Linnane of Gurtacripane? James, age 24, a "shoemaker," was the son of James Beasley of Lixnaw.

Margaret Lynan & Thomas Diggins
m. Nov. 1868 (Patrick Dillon & Mary Kennelly), Shrone, Listowel
Michael, Sept. 1871 (Mary Dwyer)
Patrick, Apr. 1875 (James Enright & Ellen Brassil)

Note: Margaret, age 30, was the daughter of Edmond Lynan of Derra. (Her name is listed as "Synon.") Thomas the son of Patrick Diggins of Curraghatoosane.

Catherine Linnane & John Harrington
Catherine, Nov. 1869 (civil record; Mary Lynch informant), Clashmelcon

Bridget Linnane & Thomas English
m. Feb. 1870 (William Linnane & John Walsh), Gullane
Jeremiah, Jan. 1871 (Bridget English)
Mary, July 1872 (Mary Lawler)
Maurice, Apr. 1875 (Bridget Flahavin)

John, May 1877 (Bridget Lawlor)
Bridget, June 1879 (Ellen English)
Edmund, Nov. 1880 (Catherine Sullivan)
Deborah, June 1883 (Patrick Moore & Mary Moore)
Catherine, Jan. 1885 (Sara Fealy)

Note: Bridget was the daughter of Maurice Linnane of Derra. Thomas was the son of Jeremiah English of Gullane.

Ellen Linnane & Michael Moriarty
m. Sept. 1870 (Timothy Linnane & Patrick King), Lisselton
Patrick, Dec. 1871 (Bridget Daughton), Loughanes
Bridget, Feb. 1875 (Joseph Linnane & Honora Quilter)
Michael, March 1876 (Sarah Linnane)
Mary, June 1879 (Mary Collins)
John, Sept. 1886 (Margaret Fealy
Joseph, Nov. 1891 (Mary O'Keefe)
Ellen, Augt. 1894 (Mary Moriarty)
Maurice Martin, Oct. 1897 (Mary Moriarty; Pat Moriarty, brother, present)

Note: Ellen, age 19, was the daughter of Joseph Linnane of Loughanes. The name was also given as "Leonard." Michael, described as a "mason" and as a "shopkeeper: was the son of Michael Moriarty of Causeway.

William Linnane & Catherine Purtill
m. Apr. 1871 (Michael O'Sullivan & Patt Hayes), Lacka
John, Dec. 1874 (Catherine Ferris)
Michael, Apr. 1877 (Hanora Purtill)
Bridget. June 1882 (Bridget Brennan)
William, Augt. 1884 (Margaret Purtill)
Hanora, Apr. 1887 (Hanora Sullivan)

Note: William was the son of Thomas Linnane & Bridget Kennelly of Lacka. Catherine was the daughter of John Purtill & Julia Connell of Ballydonohoe.

Timothy Linnane & Catherine Weeks
m. Feb. 1872 (Timothy McEssey & William Walsh), Tarbert
John, Jan. 1874 (William Weeks & Helen Kennelly)

Timothy, Feb. 1877 (John Linnane & Mary Linnane)

Note: Timothy was the son of Timothy Linnane, dec'd. Catherine was the daughter of John Weeks, dec'd. Their children immigrated to America.

Maurice Linnane & Mary Walsh
m. March 1872 (Maurice Walsh & Michael Linnane), Ballydonohoe
Maurice, March 1874 (Honora Linnane)
Johanna, Nov. 1876 (Margaret Walsh)

Note: Maurice, described as a "cooper," was the son of Maurice Linnane & Nora Purcell of Ballydonohoe. Mary was the daughter of John Walsh, dec'd., of Ballydonohoe.

William Linnane & Margaret Costello
m. Jan. 1873 (Thomas Foley & Thomas English), Derra
Maurice, Jan. 1874 (Ellen Costello)
Michael, Apr. 1877 (Hanora Purtill)
Martin, June 1878 (Mary Lawlor)
Patrick, Feb. 1881 (Patrick Breen & Joanna Quinn)
Edmond, Apr. 1883 (Deborah Mangan)
Deborah, Apr. 1885 (Catherine Tidings)
Joanna, Apr. 1888 (Joanna Denny), Trippul
Margaret, March 1891 (Catherine Walsh)

Note: William was the son of Maurice Linnane of Derra. Margaret was the daughter of Martin Costello of Derra.

Thomas Linnane & Johanna Carmody
m. Feb. 1873 (Thomas Ferris & Patrick Woulfe)
John, May 1874 (Thomas Carmody & Mary Carmody), Gortacrossane
William, July 1876 (Thomas Carmody & Ellen Carmody)
Mary, Dec. 1878 (Edmund Rahilly & Bridget Carmody)
Maurice, Jan. 1881 (Maurice Linnane & Mary Ferris), Curraghatoosane
Thomas, July 1884 (John Leonard & Honora Scanlan), Gortacrossane
Honora, May 1886 (John Linnane & Ellen Carmody)
Patrick, Apr. 1890 (William Linnane & Bridget Carmody)
James, Jan. 1894 (Michael Mulvihill & Mary Mulvihill)

Note: Thomas, age 22, was the son of John Linnane, dec'd., of? The name also appears as "Leonard." Johanna, age 22, was the daughter of Thomas Carmody of? [locations are indecipherable.]

Timothy (Thade) Linnane & Mary Rice
m. Apr. 1873 (Patrick Rice & Michael Linnane), Blanemore?
Mary, July 1874 (Catherine Rice)
Michael, Augt. 1875 (Catherine Rice), Coolkeragh
Honora, May 1876 (Johanna Stack)
Honora, Apr. 1877 (Honora Linnane)
Thomas, March 1878 (Catherine Rice)
Catherine, Augt. 1880 (Catherine Rice), Blanemore
Honora, July 1882 (Catherine Rice), Coolkeragh
Maurice, Feb. 1885 (Catherine Rice)
Joanna, May 1887 (Ellen Kissane)
Michael, Oct. 1892 (Mary Linnane), Blanemore

Note: Timothy was the son of Maurice Linnane & Honora Foley of Lacka. Mary was the daughter of William Rice & Catherine Walsh of Blanemore.

William Linnane & Bridget Sullivan
Thomas, Jan. 1874 (John Kennelly & Mary Kennelly), Letter

Ellen Linnane & Michael Ginnaw
m. Feb. 1875 (Michael Broder & Mary Keane), Listowel

Note: Ellen, age 20, was the daughter of John Linnane, dec'd., of Listowel. Michael, age 19, was the son of John Ginnaw of Listowel.

Catherine Linnane & Michael Lynch
Margaret, July 1875 (John Gleeson & Mary Gleeson), Tullahennel
Julia, Feb. 1878 (Jeremiah Molyneaux & Margaret Molyneaux)

John Linnane & Mary Allen
m. Feb. 1876 (Edmund Kissane & Margaret Kissane), Lacka
Hanora, Feb. 1877 (Bridget Callaghan; Catherine Casey, civil informant)
Patrick, May 1882 (Bridget Callaghan)
John, Nov. 1884 (Thomas Allen & Debora Gallivan)

Denis, Jan. 1887 (Ellen Healy), Killomeerhoe
James, June 1890 (John Cahill & Joanna Cahill)
Mary, June 1892 (Joanna Enright)

Note: John was the son of John Linnane of Lacka. Mary was the daughter of Denis Allen of Lahesheragh. Mary's name is also given as "Margaret."

Michael Linnane & Margaret Stack
m. Feb. 1876 (Garrett Stack & Thomas Lyons)
Catherine, Dec. 1876 (Catherine Foley; Honora Linnane, civil informant), Lacka
Mary, Dec. 1879 (Elizabeth Stack)
Margaret, March 1882 (Elizabeth Stack)

Note: Michael, age 30, was the son of Thomas Linnane of Ballybunion. Margaret, age 22, was the daughter of Michael Stack of? [indecipherable].

John Linnane & Bridget Shea
m. Nov. 1877 (Gerald Fleming & Johanna Shea), Clievragh
Mary, Dec. 1878 (James Shea & Johanna Shea)
Margaret, Sept. 1884 (James Shea & Joahnna Shea)

Note: John, age 30 and described as a widower, was the son of David Linnane, dec'd., of Listowel. Bridget, age 22, was the daughter of James Shea of Listowel.

John Linnane & Mary Fitzmaurice
m. March 1878 (Timothy Fitzmaurice & John Collins), Lacka
Honora, Feb. 1879 (Bridget Fitzmaurice)
Mary, Apr. 1880 (Johanna Connor)
Maurice, Apr. 1881 (Ellen Kissane)
Timothy, Oct. 1883 (Hanora Linnane)
John, June 1890 (Hanora Linnane)

Note: John was the son of Maurice Linnane of Lacka. Mary was the daughter of Timothy Fitzmaurice of Moybella.

Margaret Linnane & Eugene Moriarty
m. Feb. 1881 (John King & Bridget Sullivan)
Maurice, Sept. 1888 (Patrick Moriarty & Bridget Riddle), Letter

John, June 1892 (Thomas Linnane & Helen Keane)
Margaret, July 1896 (Maurice Riddle & Catherine Riddle)

Note: Margaret, age 20, was the daughter of William Linnane of Letter.
Eugene, age 26, was the son of Eugene Moriarty, dec'd., of Letter.

James Linnane & Joanna Quinn
m. Feb. 1883 (Michael Linnane & Catherine Breen), Ballydonohoe
Michael, Dec. 1883 (Honora Linnane)
Honora, Dec. 1883, Michael's twin (Mary McCarthy)
Maurice, Apr. 1885 (Margaret Fealy)
Margaret, Dec. 1887 (Honora Quinn)
John, Oct. 1889 (Catherine Cantillon)
James, Augt. 1891 (Mary Foley)

Note: James was the son of Maurice Linnane of Ballydonohoe. Joanna was
the daughter of James Quinn of Ballyconry.

Bridget Leonard & Dennis Dooling
m. June 1883 (John Walsh & Julia Scanlan), Coolard
Edmund, June 1884 (Arabella Leonard)
Mary, July 1886 (Catherine Kiely)
Daniel, July 1889 (Ellen Leonard)
Timothy, Augt. 1891 (Margaret Roche)

Note: Bridget was the daughter of Thomas Leonard of Gunsboro. Denis was
the son of Thomas Dooling, dec'd., of Coolard.

Joseph Linnane & Margaret Mulvihill
Margaret, March 1884 (Daniel Mulvihill & Margaret Mulvihill), Listowel
Parish

Sara Leonard & John Jones
m. Apr. 1884 (John Collins & John Kennelly), Lisselton Parish

Note: Sara was the daughter of Joseph Leonard, dec'd., of Ballydonohoe. John
was the son of Thomas Jones of Ballydonohoe.

Maurice Linnane & Honora Enright
m. March 1886 (John Walsh & Maurice Connor), Ballydonohoe
Joseph, Apr. 1886 (Mary Enright)

Note: Maurice was the son of Joseph Linnane, dec'd., of Lisselton. Honora
was the daughter of Timothy Enright of Ballydonohoe. The civil record has
her surname as "Kissane."

Margaret Linnane & Maurice Boyle
m. Jan 1890 (Michael O'Connor & Mary Collins)
Margaret, Feb. 1890 (Cornelius Linnane & Hanora Linnane), Kilcolman
Bridget, Apr. 1892 (Edmond McElligott & Mary McElligott)
John, Dec. 1894 (John Collins & Ellen Collins)
Catherine, July 1897 (Thomas McElligott & Alice Fahey), Curraghderrig

Note: Margaret was the daughter of William Linnane of Kilcolman. Maurice,
a "blacksmith," was the son of John Boyle of Kilcolman.

Catherine Leonard & Michael Galvin, Glouria
m. Feb. 1890 (Edmund Leonard & Catherine Kissane)

Note: Catherine was the daughter of John Leonard of Glouria. Michael was
the son of John Galvin, dec'd., of Glouria.

Edmund Leonard & Bridget Kissane
m. Feb. 1895 (William O'Sullivan & Hanora Kissane), Ballybunion Parish

Note: Edmund was the son of Thomas Leonard of Coolard. Bridget was the
daughter of John Kissane of Kilgarvin.

John Linnane & Margaret Horgan
Mary, Nov. 1895 (Honora Linnane), Glouria
John, Oct. 1897 (civil record, John Linnane, grandfather, present),
Knockenagh, Galey
Patrick, Apr. 1901 (John Linnane & Mary Linnane)

Denis Leonard & Mary Kennelly
m. Jan. 1897 (Pat O'Connor & Katie Kennelly)

Note: Denis was the son of John Leonard of Glin. Mary was the daughter of Michael Kennelly of Leitrim, Listowel.

Anabella Leonard & Timothy Lyons
m. March 1897 (John Long & Anna Lawlor), Ballybunion Parish

Note: Anabella was the daughter of Thomas Leonard of Gunsboro. Timothy was the son of Thomas Lyons of Guhard.

Mary Linnane & Maurice Moriarty
Maurice, Oct. 1897 (Mary Moriarty), Loughanes
Patrick, Sept. 1901 (James Kennelly & Mary Farrell), Listowel

John Linnane & Mary Dowling
John, Oct. 1897 (Mary Dowling), Glouria

Mary Linnane & Edmund Connor
m. May 1898 (John Kirby & John Mulvihill), Listowel Parish
Mary Ellen, July 1898 (John Mulvihill & Mary Linnane)
John Joseph, Oct. 1899 (John Linnane & Bridget Linnane)
William, Dec. 1900 (James Power & Margaret Linnane)

Note: Mary, age 20, was the daughter of John Linnane of Clievragh. Edmund, age 22, was the son of William Connor of Listowel.

Mary Linnane & William Egan
m. Feb. 1901 (John Quilty & Kate Linnane), Blanemore
Mary, Apr. 1901 (Thomas Linnane & Honora Linnane)

Note: Mary was the daughter of Timothy Linnane of Blanemore. William was the son of Thomas Egan of Tullahennel.

Maggie Linnane & John Fogarty
m. July 1903 (Timothy Fogarty & Lizzie Mary Pelican)
Honora, Sept. 1905 (Timothy Fogarty & Bridget Linnane)

Note: Maggie, age 20, was the daughter of John Linnane of Clievragh. John was the son of Patrick Fogarty, a "horse trainer," of Listowel.

Hanoria Linnane & Martin Brennan
m. July 1904 (John Walsh & William Dee)

Note: Hanoria was the daughter of John Linnane of Lacka. Martin was the son of Michael Brennan of Lacka.

Bridget Linnane & Michael Lynch
m. Nov. 1904 (Michael Boland & Sara Boland)

Note: Bridget was the daughter of William Linnane of Farranastack. Michael was the son of Michael Lynch of Farranastack.

William Leonard & Mary Prendeville
m. March 1905 (David Lawlor & John Buckley)

Note: William was the son of Simon Leonard & Catherine Barrett of Finuge. Mary was the daughter of Michael Prendeville & Ellen Sullivan of Finuge.

Thomas Linnane & Bridget Scanlan
m. Feb. 1906 (Milly Kennelly & Nora Scanlan)

Note: Thomas, age 28, was the son of Timothy Linnane of Ballybunion. Bridget, age 30, was the daughter of Daniel Scanlan of Leitrim West, Newton Sandes.

Honoria Linnane & Maurice Bambury
m. May 1907 (Michael Linnane & Mary Linnane)

Note: Honoria was the daughter of William Linnane of Lacka. Maurice was the son of Edmund Bambury of Killomeerhoe.

Hannah Linnane & Denis Buckley
m. Feb. 1909 (Denis O'Connor & Maggie Boyle)

Note: Hannah was the daughter of William Linnane of Asdee. Denis was the son of John Buckley of Asdee.

Edmond Linnane & Anne Edgworth

m. Feb. 1909 (James? & Mary Edgworth)

Note: Edmond was the son of William Linnane of Ballydonohoe. Anne was the daughter of John Edgworth of Asdee.

Katie Leonard & Michael McElligott
m. Feb. 1909 (Robert Dillon & Catherine Stack)

Note: Katie was the daughter of Michael Linnane of Lacka. Michael was the son of Michael McElligott of Bunafara?

Michael Linnane & Ellen Sullivan
m. June 1909 (Michael Linnane & Mary Linnane)

Note: Michael was the son of William Linnane of Lacka. Ellen was the daughter of Daniel Sullivan of Asdee.

William Linnane & Margaret Corridan
m. Nov. 1909 (John Linnane & Catherine Corridan)

Note: William, a "grocer," was the son of Timothy Linnane of Listowel. Margaret was the daughter of Michael Corridan of Listowel.


Civil Record of Deaths (townlands and informants are in parentheses)

Maurice Leonard, March 1879, 75, "solicitor," (the Square, Listowel, Thomas Leonard)
Maurice Linnane, Nov. 1879, 61, married, (Lacka, John Linnane)
Patrick Linnane, March 1880, 63, married, (Gortacrossane, Johanna Ferris)
Thomas Linnane, Augt. 1881, 8, (Coolard, John Linnane)
James E. Leonard, Jan. 1882, 55, married, "civil engineer," (Listowel, Daniel Linnane)
John Linnane, June 1882, 6 days, (Clievragh, John Linnane, father)
Thomas Leonard, Jan. 1883, 77, single, "gentleman," (Listowel, Daniel Linnane, brother)
Frances Linnane, Apr. 1883, 65, married, (Loughanes, Timothy Linnane, son)
Joseph Linnane, May 1883, 80, widower, (Loughanes, Tim Linnane, son)

Bridget Linnane, May 1884, 86, widow, (Kilcox, Patt Linnane, grandson)

Thad Linnane, Sept. 1884, 4, (Lacka, Mary Maloney of Lacka)

Michael Linnane, Feb. 1885, 72, married, (Addergown, Catherine Harrington, sister)

Margaret Linnane, Augt. 1885, 4, (Lacka, Honoria Linnane, grandmother)

Thomas Leonard, June 1886, 78, married, (Gunsboro, Anne Linnane)

Jane Leonard, June 1886, 62, widow of Maurice, (Listowel, Julia Murphy)

Timothy Linnane, June 1887, 22, (Lacka, Kate Purtill)

Margaret Linnane, June 1887, 80, widow, (Market St. Listowel, Patt Wilmot of Listowel)

Denis Linnane, May 1888, 15 months, (Killomeerhoe, Johanna Linnane)

Timothy Linnane, May 1889, 5 months, (Killomeerhoe, John Linnane, father)

Thomas Linnane, July 1890, 18, (Lacka, John Hinchy)

Thomas Linnane, July 1890, 18, (Kilarada?, Catherine Linnane, mother)

Mary Leonard, Dec. 1890, 81, single, "lady," (Listowel, Daniel Leonard, brother)

Deborah Linnane, Dec. 1893, 82, widow of Maurice, (Derra, Michael Linnane, grandson)

Bridget Linnane, Sept. 1894, 75, widow of Thomas, (Lacka, Catherine Linnane, d.-in-law)

William Linnane, Augt. 1896, 75, married, (Letter, John Moriarty)

Bridget Linnane, Apr. 1897, 5 months, (Clievragh, John Linnane, father)

John Linnane, July 1897, 75, single, (Addergown Cath. Harrington of Clashmelcon, sister)

Julia Leonard, Sept. 1897, 86, widow, (Ballyrehan? James Beasley)

John Linnane, Dec. 1897, 47, married (Urlee, Listowel workhouse)

Michael Linnane, March 1901, 7, (Ballydonohoe, James Linnane, father)

Honoria Linnane, Oct. 1901, 84, widow of Maurice, (Lacka, J. Linnane, grandson)

Mary Linnane, June 1904, 52, (Coolkeragh, Timothy Linnane, husband)

Kate Linnane, Sept. 1904, 76, married, (Lacka, Michael Linnane, nephew)

Michael Linnane, June 1905, 15, (Curraghatoosane Hospital)

John Leonard, Augt. 1905, 70, married, Tarbert (Curraghatoosane Hosptial)

Daniel Leonard, Nov. 1905, 81, single, "gentleman farmer," (Listow., P. Burke, nephew)

William Linnane, March 1906, 72, married, (Kilcolman, Maurice Boyle, son-in-law)

Mary Leonard, Nov. 1906, 60, single, (Hoboken, New Jersey)

Michael Leonard, Sept. 1907, 73, married, "shopkeeper," (Ballybunion, E. Forde)

John Leonard, Feb. 1908, 60, married, (Clievragh, Curraghatoosane Hospital)

Johanna Linnane, May 1910, 22, Derra, (Patrick Linnane, brother)
Margaret Linnane, Jan. 1911, 60, married, (Derra, Debbie Linnane, daughter)
Edmund Linnane, Feb. 1911, 26, single, (Derra, Debbie Linnane, sister)
Thomas Linnane, June 1911, 32, married, (Coolkeragh, Timothy Linnane, father)
Timothy Linnane, Feb. 1912, 64, widower, (Coolkeragh, Edmond Power)
Julia Leonard, March 1913, 5 months, (Patch?, Listowel, Michael Leonard, father)
John Linnane, Nov. 1913, 82, married, (Glouria, John Linnane, son)
Maurice J. Leonard, June 1914, 62, married, "gentleman," (Listowel, T. Downing)
Julia Linnane, July 1914, 90, single, (Tullahennel, Julia Lynch, niece)
Margaret Linnane, Oct. 1914, 69, (Lacka, Michael Linnane, husband)
Honoria Linnane, Dec. 1914, 74, single, (Lisselton, Curraghatoosane Hospital)
Hannah Linnane, May 1916, 30, (Lacka, Maurice Linnane, husband)
Bridget Linnane, Dec. 1917, 90, widow, (Letter, Thomas Linnane, son)
Bridget Linnane, March 1918, 80, widow, (Letter, John Buckley, son-in-law)
William Linnane, Augt. 1918, 75, widower, (Lacka, Mary Linnane, daughter-in-law)
John Linnane, May 1919, 74, married, (Lacka, Maurice Linnane, son)
Timothy Linnane, Oct. 1918, 80, single, (Listowel, Curraghatoosane Hospital)
Mary Linnane, June 1919, 71, widow of John, (Lacka, Maurice Linnane, son)
Johanna Linnane, Oct. 1920, 60, married, (Gortacrossane, Thomas Linnane, husband)


Additional Linnane Note

In Lisselton Cemetery there is a monument—"This tomb was erected by John Leonard for him and his posterity. Anno 1920."

# Laughil Townland, Kiltullagh Parish, County Roscommon, 19th Century Records

Laughil—*Leachoil* in Irish (the "half wood")—is located in Kiltullagh Parish, County Roscommon. It is a small townland situated in the hills bordering County Mayo. Total valuation in Griffith's 1857 Valuation was 28-5-0 pounds Sterling. Acreage was 81 acres, two roods and 32 perches (Irish). The Nineteenth Century landlords included the artist Roderick O'Connor.

Rundale partners in Griffith's 1857 Valuation

A. John Grennan
B. Michael Hart
C. Timothy Flynn
D. Patrick Hart
E. Connor Flynn
F. Peter Flynn
G. William Forde

Closed Valuation Book circa 1864

A. John Grennan
B. Michael Hart
C. Timothy Flynn
D. Patrick Hunt
    Patrick Fitzmaurice
E. Connor Flynn
F. Peter Flynn
G. William Forde


Closed Valuation Book after 1901
1. Stephen Grennan
2. Timothy Flynn, Jr.
3. William Forde
4. Thomas Flynn

Note: The families left of Bridget Hunt, Patrick Fitzmaurice and Michael Flynn left Laughil as part of the Congested Districts Board relocations.


Closed Valuation Books – Changes in Tenancy (note: indicated years are estimates)

A.  John Grennan
    Frances Grennan (c. 1891)
    Stephen Grennan
B.  Michael Hart
    Peter Flynn (c. 1873)
C.  Timothy Flynn
    Honor Flynn (c. 1871)
    Timothy Flynn, Jr. (c. 1880)
D.  Patrick Hart
    Patrick Hunt
    Bridget Hunt (1884)
E.  Connor Flynn
    Timothy Flynn (c. 1873)
    Thomas Flynn (c. 1910)

F.  Peter Flynn
    Michael Flynn
G.  William Forde


1901 Census

William Forde, 65
Margaret Forde (nee Hoban), 65
Bridget, 30
William, 28

Michael Flynn, 68
Bridget Flynn (nee Loftus), 63
Kate, 18
Peter, 9 (grandson)

Timothy Flynn, 70
Anne Flynn (nee Moran), 70
Thomas, 40 (widower)
Mary Hunt, 4 (granddaughter)

Timothy Flynn, Jr., 50
Catherine Flynn (nee Meehan), 45
Mary, 18
Nora, 16
Thomas, 14
Kate, 12
Ellen, 10
Tim, 8
John, 6

Stephen Grennan, 36
Nora Grennan (nee Sullivan), 38
John, 8
Kate, 6
Thomas, 2

Patrick Fitzmaurice, 70 (widower)

Bridget Hunt (nee Fitzmaurice), 75 (widow)
Patrick Hunt, 40
Bridget Hunt (nee Hussey), 37
Bridget, 8
Patrick, 7
Mary, 5
John, 5
Andrew Hubert, 4
Catherine, 2

Note: in the 1911 Census Mary is named "Kate" and is not listed as John's twin. An additional child, Margaret, was born in Dec, 1901.

<u>1911 Census</u>

William Forde, 86
Margaret Forde, 80 (married 55 years, 6 children, 5 alive)
Bridget, 43
William Forde, 40
Ellen Forde, 28 (married less than a year)

Anne Flynn, 80, widow
Thomas Flynn, 53
Mary Flynn, 56 (married 9 years, 4 children, 4 alive)
Maggie, 8
John, 1

Timothy Flynn, 61
Catherine Flynn, 59 (married 33 years, 9 children, 9 alive)
Ellen, 22
John, 18
John Conway, 6 (nephew, born in New Jersey)

Stephen Grennan, 46 married
John, 18

Kate, 16
Francis, 15
Thomas, 12

Note: Stephen's wife is not listed in the census


Kiltullagh Parish Records, Baptisms & Marriages

Martin Flatley & Catherine Harkan
Thomas, Dec. 1839 (Patrick Harkan & Bridget Burke)

Peter Flynn & Bridget Mulkean
"churching of the wife of Peter Flynn," Dec. 1839
Bridget, March 1841 (Thady Flynn & Sara Mulkean)
Patrick, Jan. 1843 (Pat Flynn & Nelly Kedian)

Catherine Fitzmorris & Hugh Murphy
m. March, 1840 (Thomas Waldron & Honor Murphy)
James, March 1841 (Thomas Fitzgerald & Ellen Fitzmaurice), Rabbitboro
Mary, Oct. 1843 (Thomas McLoughlin & Bridget Fitzmaurice)
Patrick, Apr. 1850 (Michael Fitzmorris)
Bridget, Dec. 1852 (James & Margaret Gibbons)
Kate, Apr. 1855 (Thomas Egan & Mary Murphy)
Margaret, Jan. 1858 (Terence O'Brien & Kate Waldron)
Ellen, Augt. 1863 (Pat Keane & Honor Collins)

Note: Hugh was from Rabbitborough, which is where they resided. He's listed
in Griffith's 1857 Valuation. Catherine Murphy, widow, died Augt. 1899, age
given as 82. Catherine Duffy, daughter, was the informant.

Thady Flynn & Honor Groake
Thomas, Dec. 1840 (Pat Flynn & Catherine Fitzmorris)
Patrick, July 1842 (Mary Flynn & Connor Flynn)
Honor, March 1844 (Martin Fitzmaurice & Ellen Fitzmaurice)
Catherine, July 1846 (Pat Flynn & Catherine Groake)
Timothy, Nov. 1850 (Peter & Mary Flynn)
Mary, Nov. 1852 (Catherine Burke & Thomas Frehily)

Bridget, June 1856 (Thomas Mylott & Bridget Loftus)
Thomas, July 1857 (Thomas Groake & Margaret Fitzmaurice)
Bridget, 1859 (Michael Flynn & Catherine Frehily) [year requires verification]

Margaret Fitzmorris & Michael Hart
m. Feb. 1841 (Thomas Hart & Mary Henaghen)

Note: The Parish register notes that Michael was from Bekan Parish, County Mayo.

Patrick Connelly & Catherine Devany
Mary, Apr. 1843 (Befs Devany)

Note: Patrick Connelly was from Laughil. A note in the register states "Parish of Creggs," which is located in Galway.

Daniel Connelly & Honor Grogan
Mary, Dec. 1843 (Catherine Fitzmaurice & Michael Hart)

Note: there is a record of death for Daniel Connelly in the Castlerea Workhouse in Apr. 1880. His age is given as 70, status "widower."

Patrick Fitzmaurice & Bridget Kyne (Coyne)
m. Jan. 1850 (Martin Flatley & Ellen Burke) [record needs verification]
Mary, Feb. 1861 (James Carroll & Sally Joyce)
Thomas, Dec. 1862 (Ellen Fitzmaurice)
Michael, Sept. 1865 (John & Mary Kyne; Ellen Diskin of Corrasluastia present)
Catherine, Feb. 1867 (Michael Flynn & Mary Hunt; Catherine Murphy present)
Bridget, Jan. 1869 (Michael Lyons & Mary Discon)
Ellen, Oct. 1871 (James Kilraine & Mary Discon; Catherine Murphy present)
Sarah Anne, Oct. 1873 (Thomas Winston & Bridget Fitzmaurice; Mary Fitzmaurice present)

Note: the Bekan Parish register clearly gives 1850 as the date of the marriage, but there is no record of children before Mary in 1861. There is a barely legibile record in the Annagh Parish book for the marriage of Patrick Fitzmaurice & Bridget Kyne in April 1861.

John Grennan & Fanny Hamrock
Bridget, Augt. 1852 (Martin Grennan & Ellen Hamrock)
Margaret, June 1855 (Stephen & Mary Hamrock)
Margaret, July 1857 (Stephen Hamrock & Margaret Hamrock)
John, June 1859 (Stephen Hamrock & Margaret Morris)
Fanny, July 1862 (Tim Flynn & Bridget Loftus)
Stephen, Oct. 1863 (Stephen Hamrock & Bridget Grennan)
Ellen, May 1869 (Thomas Burke & Bridget Grennan)
Martin, Oct. 1872 (John Lyons & Mary Grennan)

Note: There were Hamrock families in the adjoining County Mayo townland of Leow. James Hambrock is described as a hedge school teacher in Garranlahan in 1826.

Patrick Hunt & Bridget Fitzmaurice
m. Feb. 1853 (Peter Fitzmaurice & Bridget Loftus)
Mary, Augt. 1854 (Pat Flynn & Bridget Hunt)
Hugh, Jan. 1858 (James Cox & Ann Dodd)
Patrick, Nov. 1859 (Pat Fitzmaurice & Bridget Fitzmaurice)
Michael, Oct. 1862 (Catherine Discon)
Thomas, Jan. 1870 (Timothy & Catherine Flynn)

Note: Pat Hunt was from Annagh Parish. Mary married Thomas Forde of Derrynacong in 1884. Patrick married Celia (or Bridget) Hussey of Clydagh in 1892. Michael married Bridget Ganley of Tully in 1890.

Timothy Flynn & Anne Moran
m. Feb. 1854 (Michael Flynn & Mary Prenty?)
John, May 1856 (Bridget Loughlin? & Catherine Flynn)
Honoria, Feb. 1858 (Thomas Waldron & Bridget Cosgrove)
Bridget, Feb. 1859 (Thady Flynn & Bridget Lyons)
"churched wife of Timothy Flynn," Feb. 1859
Honoria, Feb. 1861 (John & Honor Neenane?)
Mary Anne, May 1863 (Mary Naughten)
Connor, June 1865 (H? & Fanny Hamrock)
Catherine, July 1867 (Michael Flynn & Mary Rogers)
Margaret Agnes, June 1869 (John & Bridget Waldron; Bridget Flynn present)
Timothy Michael, 1873 (John & Bridget Flynn; Bedelia Flynn present)

Note: Timothy Flynn was described as a shoemaker and farmer. Anne Moran was from Annagh Parish.

Michael Flynn & Mary Fleming
m. March 1855 (Andrew Breheny & Anne Brady)
"churched wife of Michael Flynn," Oct. 1856
John, Jan. 1858 (Connor Flynn & Kate Flynn)
Peter, June 1861 (Peter Flynn & Bridget Frehily)
Michael, July 1863 (Peter Flynn & Margaret Hoban)

William Forde & Margaret Hoban
m. Dec. 1856 (Patrick Johnson & Mary Reily)
Mary, Sept. 1857 (Pat Hoban & Kate Forde)
Thomas, Jan. 1860 (Thomas Hoban & Margaret Hoban)
Catherine, Dec. 1862 (Thomas Hoban & Bridget Fitzmaurice)
"churched Mrs. William Forde," Nov. 1866
Bridget, Sept. 1869 (Pat Forde & Catherine Frehily; Mary Forde of Laughil present)
William, Sept. 1872 (Peter Flynn & Mary Killian)

Note: Margaret Hoban was from Bekan Parish.

Charles Kelly & Mary Loftus
m. Jan. 1862 (James Cruise? & Ellen Hoban)
Hugh, Sept. 1870 (John Kelly? & Bridget Fitzmaurice), Annagh Parish

Michael Flynn & Bridget Loftus
m. Apr. 1867 (Timothy Flynn & Honoria Flynn)
James, Augt. 1868 (Peter Flynn & Mary Fitzmaurice; Margaret Loftus present)
Patrick, Sept. 1870 (Charles Kelly & Mary Forde)
Bridget, Oct. 1872 (Charles Kelly & Mary Hart)
Margaret, Oct. 1876 (John Grennan & Catherine Forde)
Mary, Oct. 1879 (Bernard Rogers & Mary Grennan)
Catherine, March 1884 (civil record)

Note: Michael was the son of Peter Flynn of Laughil. Bridget was the daughter of John Loftus, dec'd., of Laughil.

Thomas Griffin & Bridget Grennan
m. Jan. 1872 (Thomas Walsh & Mary Anne Browne)
Michael, Nov. 1876 (civil record, Mary Griffin present), Meelickroe

Note: Bridget was the daughter of John Grennan of Laughil. Thomas was the son of Michael Griffin, dec'd., of Meelickroe. There is a civil death record for Thomas Griffin of Meelickroe, age 55, in Dec. 1883.

Timothy Flynn & Catherine Meehan (Meath)
m. March 1878 (Thomas Flynn & Bridget Plunkett), Ballyhaunis
Michael, Feb. 1879 (Michael Meehan & Bridget Flynn)
Bridget, July 1880 (John Murry & Bridget Meehan)
Maria, Jan. 1882 (civil record)
Honoria, June 1883 (civil record)
Kate, Feb. 1887 (civil record, Fanny Grennan present)
Ellen, Feb. 1889 (civil record)
Timothy, Nov. 1890 (civil record)
John, Dec. 1892 (civil record)

Note: Timothy was the son of Timothy Flynn, dec'd., of Laughil. Catherine was the daughter of John Meath of Leow. The name is given as "Meath" in the marriage record and as "Meehan" in the civil record of births. The civil record of the birth of their son Thomas was not found. John married Bridget Carney in Knock Parish in Dec. 1930.

Ellen Grennan & John Kearins
m. May 1888 (Stephen Hamrock & Bridget Forde)

Note: Ellen was the daughter of John Grennan of Laughil. John was the son of Bernard Kearins of Leow.

Stephen Grennan & Honor Sullivan
m. March 1892 (Martin Grennan & Kate Meehan), Ballyhaunis
John, Apr. 1893 (civil record)
Kate, June 1894 (civil record, Frances Grennan informant)
Francis, Jan. 1897 (civil record)

Note: Stephen was the son of John Grennan, dec'd., of Laughil. Honor was the daughter of Thomas Sullivan of Derrylea. No civil record has been located for their son, Thomas.

Thomas Flynn & Mary Scally
m. June 1902 (John Winston & Bridget Scally), Aghamore Parish

Note: Thomas was the son of Timothy Flynn of Laughil. Mary was the daughter of John Scally, also of Laughil?

William Forde & Ellen Noonan
m. March 1911 (John Grennan & Mary Byrne), Ballyhaunis

Note: William was the son of William Forde & Margaret Hoban of Laughil. Ellen was the daughter of Patrick Noonan of Tullaghane in Annagh Parish.

<u>Laughil Deaths – Civil records</u> (informants are in parentheses)

Thomas Hunt, Nov. 1871, 2, son of Patrick & Bridget Hunt
Hanoria Flynn, March 1878, 26, single, (Honor Flynn)
Patrick Hunt, Apr. 1884, 53, married, (Catherine Fitzmaurice)
John Grennan, Jan. 1889, 60, married, (Martin Grennan, son)
Fanny Grennan, Dec. 1896, 58, widow, (Stephen Grennan, son)
Margaret Hart, March 1899, 92, widow, (Bridget Flynn, daughter)
Timothy Flynn, Dec. 1910, 86, married, (Mary Flynn, daughter-in-law)
Patrick Fitzmaurice, March 1911, age 79, widower, (Moigh, Mary Murray, niece)
[This is the only reference to Patrick Fitzmaurice in the Castlerea Union in this time period.]
William Forde, Sept. 1915, 78, married, (William Forde, son)
Margeret Forde, Apr. 1916, 75, widow, (William Forde, son)
Bridget Hunt, died Sept. 1917, 91, widow of Patrick, (Milltown, Patrick Hunt, son)
Anne Flynn, Nov. 1921, 94, widow of Timothy, (Thomas Flynn, son)
Timothy Flynn, May 1924, 73, spouse of Catherine Meehan, (John Flynn, son)
Catherine Flynn, Dec. 1934, 85, widow of Timothy, (John Flynn, son)

<u>In Garranlahan Churchyard</u>:

"In loving memory of Timothy Flynn, died 1911 / Connor Flynn, died 1921"
[Connor Flynn was one year, Margaret Flynn, sister, informant]

"In loving memory of Thomas Flynn / Laughil, died 1932 / his wife Mary /
died 1938 / and daughter Bridget / died 1972 / son Connor (no date)" [records
require verification]

<u>Petty Court Records</u>

[By permission of: Transcripts (c) IIMI & FMP, Images (c) NAI, available
on Findmypast]

Note: complainants are listed first, defendants second. Unless other specified,
all individuals were from Laughil. The date indicated may refer to the date of
the infraction or to the court date.

Michael Hart vs. John Grennan. Trepass of defendant's cow and ass on
complainant's grass. 9 Nov. 1853.

William Forde vs. Bridget Loftus and Mary Lyons. Entering complainant's
house and taking a pot and four pounds Sterling. 1 Nov. 1855.

William Forde vs. Michael Flynn & Peter Flynn. Assault. Defendants fined five
shillings, court costs three shilling, imprisoned for one fortnight. 4 Apr. 1860.

Michael Flynn vs. Henry Hamrock, James Hamrock, & Mary Anne Hamrock
of Leow. Assault. 17 March 1867.

Henry Hamrock of Leow vs. Michael Flynn, Bridget Loftus, Honoria Flynn
& Timothy Flynn. Assault. 17 March 1867.

Peter Flynn vs. William Forde & Margaret Forde. Trepass of defendants'
cows onto complainant's oats. Fined one shilling for oats, one shilling court
costs. 29 May 1868.

William Forde, John Grennan, Patrick Hunt, Patt Fitzmaurice, & Honor Flynn vs. Thady Flynn. Unlawfully taking possession of land and a portion of bog and preventing complainants from taking "bog stuff for manure." 4 Nov. 1868.

Bridget Hunt vs. Thady Flynn. "Forcibly and unlawfully taking away four stocks of oats." 14 Oct. 1872.

John Grennan vs. Thady Flynn & Thomas Flynn. Assault. 2 May 1882.

John Grennan vs. Thady Flynn, Thomas Flynn, & Anne Flynn. Unlawfully preventing public passage. 2 May 1882.

John Grennan vs. Thady Flynn, Thomas Flynn, & Anne Flynn. Assault, "having cruelly beat and knocked down complainant." Punishment in default of payment, county jail for seven? days. 2 May 1882.

Tim Flynn vs. Thady Flynn. Assault and unlawfully preventing passage to his land. 13 Apr. 1883.

John Grennan vs. Anne Flynn, Tim Flynn, & Connor Flynn. Assault. Fined in lieu of prison. 19 May 1883.

Thady Flynn vs. John Grennan, Ellen Grennan, Stephen Grennan, Fanny Grennan. Assault. 20 May 1883.

Connor Flynn vs. Stephen Grennan. Assault. 20 May 1883.

Tim Flynn Jr. vs. Anne Flynn & Thomas Flynn. Assault. Case withdrawn. 1 Feb. 1884.

Timothy Flynn vs. Thomas Flynn. Assault and "wantonly striking the complainant's ass." 6 Feb. 1884.

Daniel Quinn of Castlerea vs Thady Flynn & Honoria Flynn. Unlawfully carried away a quantity of hay seized by complainant by virtue of a court decree at Corrasluastia. 23 Sept. 1885.

Mary Sheridan vs. Anne Flynn of Laughil. Threatening and abusive language, "putting complainant in terror," at the Ballinlough railroad station. 18 June 1886.

The Queen vs. James Flynn of "Loughill." Assault of Constable Alex Cruickshanks on a public street in Ballyhaunis. 19 Feb. 1891.

The Queen vs. Rose White, publican, of Ballinlough, Thady Flynn of Laughil, Peter Flynn of Clydagh and Patrick Rogers of Clydagh. Her licensed premises opened for the sale of intoxicating drink on a Sunday. 11 June 1893.

Constable Donegan vs. Timothy Flynn. Intoxicated on the public street in Ballinlough. 1 Feb. 1901.

# Derrynacong Townland, Annagh Parish, County Mayo, 19ᵗʰ Century Records

*For Kathleen Fitzharris, RIP*

Annagh Parish, South Mayo Parliamentary District, Loughanboy Electoral District, Claremorris Poor Law Union, Costello Barony

From *Doire na conga* – "strip of oak wood"

19ᵗʰ Century landlords – the various Viscount Dillon

Lease 1794 (Viscount Dillon)

Thomas Boland & Co.

Tithe Payers 1830

Thomas Boland & Co.

Thomas Kelly & Co.

## Tithe Applotment Book 1835

Thomas Boland & Co.

## 1841 House Valuation Book

Michael Kedian – 4 pounds rate for home with projection in rear, barn and stable

## Griffith's valuation 1856 (Ordnance Survey map #93)

Note: Holdings are in rundale. "Office" indicates an additional structure such as a barn or shed.

1a) Patrick Kedian (land, house & office) 80 acres
    b) Peter Connell (land, house & office)
    c) John Waldron (land & house)
    d) James Kelly (land, house & office)
    e) Patrick Fitzmaurice, "widow" (land & house)

2a) John Fitzmaurice (of #6, land, house & office) 54 acres
    b) Patrick Forde (of #6, land & house)
    c) Patrick Fitzmaurice (of #6, land & house)
    d) William Quinn (land & house)

3a) Michael Kedian (of #4 & #7, land, house & offices) 53 acres
    b) Thomas Hunt (land, house & offices)
    c) Mary Hunt (land & house)

4) Michael Kedian (land) 6 acres

5) James Hunt (of #7, land & house) 7 acres

6) Patrick Forde (land) 7 acres
    John Fitzmaurice (land)

Patrick Fitzmaurice (land)
Patrick Fitzmauruce, "widow" (land)

7) Michael Kedian (land, bog) 13 acres
James Hunt (land, bog)

8a) Mark Dyer (land, house & offices) 34 acres
  b) Thomas Frehily (land, house & office)
  c) Martin Dyer (land & house)

9) Patrick Boland (land, house & offices) 23 acres

10) Nappy Boland (land, house & office) 26 acres

11a) Martin Waldron (land, house & office) 21 acres
  b) Patrick Kearns (land, house & office)
  c) John Grogan (land & house)
  d) Martin Waldron, Jr. (gardens & house)


## Manuscript Map 1858

Note: Between 1856 – 1858 the rundale holdings were divided into individual properties. Measurements are in chains and perches. English units.

1. John Waldron
0-3-15 arable, 5-0-6 reclaimed, no bottom land
2-0-18 reclaimable, 2-3-23 bog, 10-2-23 total

2. Peter Connell
0-1-30 arable, 2-2-4 reclaimed, 2-1-2 bottom land
3-1-15 reclaimable, no bog, 8-2-1 total

3. Patrick Kedian
4-0-0 arable, 1-3-30 reclaimed, 1-3-23 bottom land
3-3-22 reclaimable, 1-3-25 bog, 13-2-20 total

4. James Kelly
3-3-14 arable, 5-3-26 reclaimed, 4-0-17 bottom land

0-3-8 reclaimable, no bog, 14-2-25 total

5.  Patrick Fitzmaurice
    2-3-25 arable, 0-0-15 reclaimed, 1-1-16 bottom land
    3-3-6 reclaimable, 0-0-30 bog, 8-1-12 total

6.  William Quinn
    0-3-20 arable, no reclaimed, 0-1-5 bottom land
    0-2-26 reclaimable, 0-2-0 bog, 2-1-11 total

7.  Patrick Forde
    3-3-39 arable, no reclaimed, 1-3-10 bottom land
    1-0-15 reclaimable, 4-0-19 bog, 11-0-3 total

8.  Michael Kedian
    9-3-27 arable, no reclaimed, 4-0-36 bottom land
    0-3-20 reclaimable, 11-2-28 bog, 26-2-31 total

9.  Thomas Hunt
    2-0-25 arable, no reclaimed, 0-2-31 bottom land
    no reclaimable, 3-2-20 bog, 6-1-36 total

10. James Cox
    1-0-28 arable, 0-0-32 reclaimed, 0-0-20 bottom land
    no reclaimable, 2-1-16 bog, 3-3-16 total

11. John Fitzmaurice
    5-3-31 arable, 0-3-23 reclaimed, 0-3-31 bottom land
    6-1-27 reclaimable, 4-1-5 bog, 18-1-37 total

12. Patrick Fitzmaurice
    4-1-4 arable, 0-0-29 reclaimed, 0-0-25 bottom land
    3-1-11 reclaimable, 0-0-25 bog, 8-0-14 total

13. Thomas Frehily
    5-0-11 arable, 1-2-0 reclaimed, 0-0-15 bottom land
    2-2-24 reclaimable, no bog, 9-1-10 total

14. Martin Dyer
    5-1-16 arable, 1-1-0 reclaimed, no bottom land
    no reclaimable, 3-0-37 bog, 9-3-13 total

15. James Hunt
    3-3-28 arable, no reclaimed, no bottom land
    0-1-20 reclaimable, 5-1-14 bog, 9-2-22 total

16. Patrick Boland
    6-2-1 arable, 1-0-16 reclaimed, 0-2-21 bottom land
    1-2-26 reclaimable, 4-3-25 bog, 14-3-9 total

17. William Boland
    6-0-29 arable, 0-1-29 reclaimed, 0-2-11 bottom land
    0-1-18 reclaimable, 3-1-24 bog, 12-3-31 total

18. Patrick Kerins
    3-3-20 arable, 0-1-15 reclaimed, 0-1-11 bottom land
    0-0-6 reclaimable, 1-3-15 bog, 6-1-37 total

19. Martin Waldron
    3-2-39 arable, 0-1-1 reclaimed, 0-0-32 bottom land
    0-0-13 reclaimble, 2-1-29 bog, 6-2-34 total


Closed Valuation Book circa 1862

Note: Valuations are in British pounds. Measurements are in English units.

1a. John Waldron, 16-3-27 acres
    1-10-0 land, 0-5-0 house, 1-15-0 valuation

2a. Peter Connell, 14-1-27 acres
    1-0-0 land, 0-5-0 house, 1-5-0 valuation

3a. Patrick Kedian, 22-3-25 acres
    3-0-0 land, 0-10-0 house, 3-10-0 valuation

3b.  Patrick Fitzmaurice (Pat, #12)
0-5-0 house, 0-5-0 valuation

4a.  James Kelly & Patrick Kedian, 24-3-30 acres
Kelly: 4-10-0 land, 0-10-0 house, 5-0-0 valuation
Kedian: 1-10-0 land, 1-10-0 valuation

5.  Patrick Fitzmaurice, 14-1-17 acres
1-17-0 land, 0-3-0 house, 2-8-0 valuation

6.  James Quinn, 3-3-33 acres
0-10-0 land, 0-2-0 house, 0-12-0 valuation

7.  Patrick Forde, 17-3-16 acres
2-15-0 land, 0-5-0 house, 3-0-0 valuation

8a.  Michael Kedian, 42-3-30 acres
6-0-0 land, 0-10-0 house, 6-10-0 valuation

8b.  Thomas Hunt (see #9)
0-5-0 house, 0-5-0 valuation

8c.  James Cox (see #10)
0-2-0 house, 0-2-0 valuation

9.  Thomas Hunt, 10-2-0 acres
1-2-0 land, 1-2-0 valuation

10.  James Cox, 7-1-20 acres
0-13-0 land, 0-13 valuation

11.  John Fitzmaurice, 32-3-15 acres
4-5-0 land, 0-10-0 house, 4-15-0 valuation

12.  Patrick Fitzmaurice (Pat), 16-1-17 acres
2-5-0 land, 2-5-0 valuation

13.  Thomas Frehily, 14-2-27 acres
3-2-0 land, 0-8-0 house, 3-10-0 valuation

14a. Martin Dyer, 16-1-13 acres
   3-0-0 land, 0-10-0 house, 3-10-0 valuation

14b. Mark Dyer
   0-5-0 house, 0-5-0 valuation

15. James Hunt, 8-2-20 acres
   1-12-0 land, 0-8-0 house, 2-0-0 valuation

16. Patrick Boland, 25-1-27 acres
   3-17-0 land, 0-8-0 house, 4-5-0 valuation

17. William Boland, 19-3-27 acres
   4-5-0 land, 0-5-0 house, 4-10-0 valuation

18a. Patrick Kearns, 22-0-11 acres
   2-2-0 land, 0-6-0 house, 2-8-0 valuation

18b. Martin Waldron, 22-0-11 acres
   1-15-0 land, 0-5-0 house, 2-0-0 valuation


Closed Valuation Books – Changes in Tenancy (note: indicated years are estimates)

Years listed in parentheses should be considered approximate dates.

1.  John Waldron
    Austin Waldron (1900)
    John Connally

2.  Peter Connell
    Reps. of Peter Connell (1903)
    James Connell
    Nora Kearns

3.  Patrick Kedian
    Peter Kedian (1903)
    Michael Kelly (1920)

3b. Patrick Fitzmaurice (1860s - 1885)

4.  James Kelly
    John Kelly (1877)
    Patrick Tully (1893)

5.  Patrick Fitzmaurice ("Widow" crossed out)
    Peter Fitzmaurice
    Patrick Fitzmaurice
    James Waldron
    Margaret Waldron
    Michael Waldron (1913)

6.  William Quinn
    James Quinn (1862)
    John Quinn
    Patrick Hanlon
    William Fitzharris

7.  Patrick Forde
    Reps. of Patrick Forde
    Thomas Forde (1894)
    Delia Forde (1939 – 1944)
    James McGarry (1944 – 1987)
    Thomas Ronayne

8a. Michael Kedian
    Patrick Kedian (1884)
    James Eddy Kedian (1914)

8b. Thomas Hunt (1860s – 1874)

8c. James Cox
    Bridget Cox (1886 – 1903)

9.  Thomas Hunt
    William Hunt (1974)
    Patrick Dyer (1907)

10. Mary Hunt
    James Cox
    Bridget Cox (1886)
    John Deasy (1900 – listed as Reps. of Bridget Cox)

11. John Fitzmaurice (Note: it appears father and son had same name.)

12. Patrick Fitzmaurice (Pat)
    Mary Regan (1913)

13. Thomas Frehily
    Reps. of Thomas Frehily (1882)
    Patrick Kenny

14a. Martin Dyer
    Reps. of Martin Dyer
    James Murphy (1900 – listed as subtenant for life to Michael Dyer)
    Reps. of James Murphy
    John Freely (1910)
    Patrick Freely (1915)

14b. Mark Dyer (1860)

15. Bridget Boland
    James Hunt
    Thomas Hunt (1900, listed as Reps. of Patrick Boland, deceased)
    Anne Hunt (1910)

16. Patrick Boland
    Bridget Boland (1885)
    William Boland (1903)
    Reps. of Thomas Ganley (1917)

17. Nappy Boland
    William Boland

18a. Patrick Kearns (1860s - 1892)
    Ellen Ganley (1900, listed as Reps. of Patrick Kearns)

James Ganley
Reps. of Thomas Ganley (1910)

18b. Martin Waldron
James Waldron
Michael Caulfield (1900, listed as Reps. of James Waldron)

19. James Hunt
Reps. of James Hunt
Thomas J. Hunt (1900, listed as Reps. of James Hunt)
Michael F. Hunt (1917)

---

<u>1841 population</u>
25 occupied houses with a population of 132

<u>1851 population</u>
22 occupied houses with a population of 104

<u>1901 population</u>
19 occupied houses with a population of 97

<u>1911 population</u>
18 occupied houses with a population of 106

---

<u>1901 Census (31 March)</u>

Austin Waldron, 60
Catherine Waldron, 60
Maggie, 32

Peter Connell, 70, widower

Peter Kedian, 40
Lizzie Kedian, 28?
John, 14
Celia, 10

Nora, 8?

Pat Tully, 32
Anne Tully, 31
Catherine, 3
Michael, 2
Bridget 2 mos?
Annie Griffin, 35, sister-in-law

James Waldron, 56
Catherine Waldron, 50
Delia, 23
John, 20
James, 18
Katie, 16
Norah, 14
Patrick, 12
Mary Fitzmaurice, 70, mother-in-law, widow

John Quinn, 55
Catherine Quinn, 45
Katie, 9

Thomas Forde, 40
Bridget Forde, 35
Mary Ellen, 13
Patrick, 10
Delia, 7
Kate, 7
Anne, 2
Honoria, 1

Patrick Kedian, 55
Bridget Kedian, 52
Delia, 16
Ellen, 13
James E., 10

William Hunt, 65, cattle dealer
Mary Hunt, 60
Bridget Lyons, 27, daughter
John, 25
Kate, 22
Mary, 20
Thomas 17

John Deasy (Dacey), 38
Mary Deasy, 37
Thomas, 10
Patrick, 9
Bridget, 6
Mary Kate, 9 mos.

John Fitzmaurice, 80
Mary Fitzmaurice, 67
John, 30
Martin, 27
Mary, 25

Michael Regan, 40
Mary Regan, 37
Pat, 8
Mary, 5
Michael, 3
Patrick Fitzmaurice, 76, father-in-law, widower

Patrick Kenny, 59
Mary Kenny, 57
Thomas, 22

Thomas Hunt, 49
Mary Hunt, 45
Patrick, 16
Honoria, 15
Michael 13
Thomas, 9

Thomas Hunt, 30
Anne Hunt, 25
Patrick, 6
John, 4
Katie, 2
Bridget Boland, 62, mother-in-law, widow

Thomas Ganley (Ganly), 32
Ellen Ganley, 35
Annie, 4
Kate, 2
Ellen, 4 mos.
Richard Fillins?, 13, servant
William Boland, 65, father-in-law

James Ganley (Ganly), 38
Ellen Ganley, 40
John Kearns, 12? (listed as son)
Michael, 9
Kate, 7
James, 3

Michael Caulfield, 36
Mary Caulfield, 30
Maggie, 1
Margaret Waldron, 69, widow

Mary Dyer, 80, widow

1911 Census (29 Apr.)

Austin Waldron, 69, widower
John Connolly, 39 son-in-law
Maggie Connolly, 36
Nellie, 5
Maggie, 4
Patrick, 1
Delia Connolly, 5, visitor

(stable, cow house, piggery, barn, shed)
Austin – 1 child, 1 alive
John & Maggie married 8 years, 3 children, 3 alive

Peter Kedian, 68
Lizzie Kedian, 38
(stable, cow house, piggery, barn, shed)
married 17 years, no children

Patrick Tully, 44
Anne Tully, 44
Kate, 13
Michael, 12
Bridget, 11
James, 8
Stephen, 3
(stable, cow house, shed)
married 15 years, 5 children, 5 alive

James Waldron, 67
Catherine Waldron, 64
Delia Grogan, 34, daughter
James, 27
Patrick, 21
James Anthony Grogan, 5 grandson
Catherine Grogan, 3, granddaughter
(two stables, cow house, piggery, barn, shed)
James & Catherine married 35 years, 7 children, 7 alive
Delia married 8 years, 3 children, 2 alive

John Quinn, 73
Catherine Quinn, 70
Kate, 19
(cow house)
married 46 years, 5 children, 2 alive

Thomas Forde, 57
Bridget Forde, 46

Nora, 11
Rose, 9
Agnes, 7
(cow house, piggery, barn, shed)
married 13 years, 4 children, 4 alive

Note: this property had a lime kiln. Anne Forde, age 13, was at her grandparents Lyons's home in Larganboy during the census.

Patrick Kedian, 70
Bridget Kedian, 65
James E., 20
Delia, 24
(stable, cow house)
married 44 years, 10 children, 8 alive

William Hunt, 80
Mary Hunt, 65
John, 32
Thomas M., 26
Mary, 28
Delia Kelly, 14, visitor, b. Co. Galway
(stable, cow house, barn, shed)
married 40 years, 5 children, 5 alive

John Deasy, 50
Mary Deasy, 52
Thomas, 20
Patrick, 17
Bridget, 16
Mary Kate, 10
Michael, 7
(cow house, piggery, shed)
married 21 years, 7 children, 5 alive

John Fitzmaurice, 45
Ellen Fitzmaurice, 39
Mary A., 7

John, 5
Bridget, 4
Helena, 2
Rosie Anne, 1
Mary Fitzmaurice, 76, mother, widow
Mary Fitzmaurice, 39, sister
(Stable, cow house, piggery, barn, shed)
married 9 years, 5 children, 5 alive

Michael Regan, 55
Mary Regan, 53
Patrick, 18
Mary, 16
Michael, 12
(cow house, shed)
married 21 years, 3 children, 3 alive

James Kenny, 39
Ellen Kenny, 34
James, 4
Mary, 3
Patrick Kenny, 79, father, widower
(stable, cow house, piggery, barn)
married 5 years, 2 children, 2 alive

John Murphy, 40
Ellen Murphy, 40
James, 7
Bridget 11
Mary, 9
Catherine, 5
Ellen, 4
Hanoria, 3
(stable, cow house, piggery, barn, shed)
married 13 years, 6 children, 6 alive

Thomas Hunt, 58
Mary Hunt, 57

Michael Francis, 23
Nora, 22
Thomas, 19
(stable, cow house, piggery, fowl house, shed)
married 27 years, 4 children, 3 alive

Bridget Boland, 80, widow,
Anne Hunt, 35, daughter-in-law, widow
Patrick, 14
John, 13
Kate, 10
Bridget, 7
Annie Mary, 4
(stable, cow house, piggery, fowl house, barn)
Anne married 12 years, 5 children, 5 alive

Thomas Ganley, 42
Ellen Ganley, 50
Annie Maria, 14
Katie, 12
Bridget Josephine, 7
(stable, cow house, piggery, barn, shed)
married 16 years, 5 children, 5 alive

James Ganley, 49
Ellen Ganley, 59
Michael, 18
Kate, 15
James, 14
Patrick, 12
Peter, 10
(stable, cow house, piggery, barn, shed)
married 20 years, 8 children, 8 alive

Michael Caulfield, 55
Mary Caulfield, 53
Margaret, 11
Martin, 9

Mary Anne, 6
James, 3
(cow house, piggery, shed)
married 12 years 4 children, 4 alive


Annagh Parish Registers, Baptisms & Marriages

Patrick Fitzmaurce & Mary Waldron
m. Apr. 1846 (John Fitzmaurice & Mary Waldron)
"Churched wife of Pat Fitzmaurice," Oct. 1852
Mary, Nov. 1852 (John Kelly & Bridget Waldron)
Judith, Nov. 1856 (Michael & Margaret Fitzmaurice)
Bridget, 1859 (Pat Bones &? Bones)
Patrick, Feb. 1866 (civil record)
Honoria, Nov. 1868 (civil record)

Note: Mary was the daughter of Patrick Waldron of Brackloon. Marriage record is in the Bekan Parish Book.

Peter Connell & Mary Morraly
Certificate to marry outside Annagh Parish, Jan. 1852
"Churched Peter's wife," Apr. 1853
Mary, Nov. 1855 (Michael Connell & Bridget Kedian)
Ellen, Dec. 1858 (Ed Connell & Bridget Smith)
Edmond, July 1864 (civil record)

John Waldron & Mary (Margaret) Grealy
m. Feb. 1852 (Martin Waldron & Mary Geraghty) [record needs verification]
Mary, March 1866 (civil record)

Peter Flynn & Mary Hunt
m. Nov. 1852 (Patrick Kelly & Mary Hunt), Clooncrim, Kiltullagh Parish
Anne, Sept. 1853 (Mary Hunt)
Bridget, Feb. 1855 (James Gannon & Anne Hunt)

Note: Mary Hunt was from Derrynacong.

Patrick Grogan & Mary Fitzmaurice
James, March 1853 (Mary Waldron)

Patrick Forde & Bridget Freeman
Michael, June 1853 (John Freely? & Catherine Dyer)
Thomas, July 1856 (Henry & Anne Hamrock)
Hubert, June 1858 (Mary Hunt)

John Waldron & Judy Grogan
John, Sept. 1853 (Honor Waldron)

Churched wife of Patrick Cadian, Sept. 1853

Michael Finnegan – marriage certificate, Feb. 1853

John Fitzmaurice – marriage certificate, 1854

James Cox & Bridget Hunt
m. Dec. 1854 (John Cox & Bridget Geraghty)
Thomas, Nov. 1855 (Pat Hunt & Mary Cox)
child, Augt. 1858 (Hugh Cox & Bridget Fitzmaurice)
child, March 1860 (no godparents listed)
Margaret, Dec. 1864 (civil record)
Bridget, Augt. 1867 (civil record, Mary Hunt of Bargarriff present)
Kate, May 1881 (John Cox & Bridget Hunt)

Patrick Fitzmaurice & Mary Bride
Thomas, Jan. 1856 (Martin & Margaret Bride)
Mary, 1860 (Peter Fitzmaurice & Kate Killean)
Michael, Feb. 1865 (Thomas Killean & Anne Killean)
Patrick, Sept. 1868 (Thomas Killeen & Anne Killeen of Corafsarce?)

William Boland & Anne Healy
Eleanor, June 1858 (Denis Healy)
Thomas, Feb. 1860 (Margaret Boland)
Patrick, Oct. 1865 (civil record)
Anne, March 1869 (Austin & Celia Caulfield)
Stephen, July 1871 (Stephen Healy & Mary Dwyer)

Catherine, Nov. 1873 (Pat & Honoria Waldron)
Mary, Augt. 1876 (Pat & Celia Boland)

Thomas Kelly & Mary Hunt
m. Jan. 1859 (J. Kelly & Mary Drudy), Killunagher
Bridget, Augt. 1864 (civil record, Thomas Hunt, grandfather, present))
Mary, July, 1866 (civil record)
Michael, Oct. 1868 (civil record, Anne Higgins of Killunagher present)

Mary was the daughter of Thomas Hunt of Derrynacong.

Patrick Kelly & Sarah Fitzmaurice
m. Jan. 1865 (Thomas Flatley & Bridget Flatley)

Note: Patrick Kelly, 38 years of age, was the son of John Kelly of Derrynacong.
Sarah Fitzmaurice was the daughter of John Fitzmaurice of Lisbane.

Patrick Kenny & Mary Frehily (Freely)
m. Feb. 1865 (David Jordan & Julia Moran)
Mary Anne, Feb. 1866 (civil record)
Patrick, Dec. 1867 (civil record)
John, Feb. 1870 (Tom Hunt & Mary Mulkeen)
James, June 1872 (David Waldron & Margaret Bridge?)
Bridget, Nov. 1874 (Martin & Bridget Co-?)
Thomas, March 1877 (Thomas Freely & Bridget Mulkeen)
Thady, Feb. 1880 (Patrick & Mary Anne Kenny)

Note: Patrick Kenny was the son of John Kenny of Cappagh. Mary Frehily
was the daughter of Thomas Frehily of Derrynacong. Bridget and Thady
immigrated to New York City.

Patrick Boland & Bridget McGuire
Mary, Nov. 1865 (civil record)
Thomas, Feb. 1871 (N. McGuire & Mary Murphy)
Anne, Dec. 1874 (Stephen & Bridget Boland)

John Fitzmaurice & Mary Grealy
Patrick, Feb. 1867 (civil record)

John, Sept. 1867 (civil record, Honoria Waldron of Derrynacong present)
Ellen, May 1869 (Thomas Ryan? & Winifred Waldron)
Martin, June 1871 (Michael & Mary Fitzmaurice)
Mary, Augt. 1873 (Pat & Mary Fitzmaurice)
Honoria, March 1876 (Pat & Mary Fitzmaurice

Note: John was the son of Martin Fitzmaurice of Derrynacong. He had two brothers: Michael, who married Anne Lyons of Spaddagh, and Patrick, who married Ellen Dwyer of Gorteen Beg in April 1857.

John Kelly & Ellen Snee
Ellen, March, 1866 (civil record)
Mary, Feb. 1868 (civil Record)
Lackey, Feb. 1870 (civil record)

Note: It is likely John & Ellen had an additional daughter, Margaret, born c. 1862.

Mary Kedian & Patrick Hussy
m. Feb. 1867 (Michael Lyons & Catherine McGarry)

Note: Mary was the daughter of Michael Kedian of Derrynacong. Patrick was the son of Patrick Hussy of Clydagh, Kitullagh Parish. They resided in Clydagh.

Patrick Kedian & Bridget Lyons
m. Feb. 1869 (John Hunt & Mary Gribbin)
James, Nov. 1871 (Michael & Mary Kedian)
Mary, Dec. 1872 (Edward & Mary Lyons)
Kate, Feb. 1875 (Thomas & Celia Lyons; Bridget Dyer of Brackloon present)
Michael, Feb. 1877 (Pat Belia & Bridget Kedian)
Cecilia, Sept. 1878 (Edward & Celia Lyons)
Thomas, Augt. 1880 (Michael Tully & Catherine Doherty)
Bridget, Oct. 1882 (Timothy & Kate Fitzmaurice)
Patrick, Nov. 1884 (Edward Dyer & Mary Fitzmaurice)

Note: Patrick Kedian was the son of Michael Kedian of Derrynacong. Bridget Lyons was the daughter of Thomas Lyons of Gurrane.

Michael Gormley & Bridget Waldron
m. March 1870 (Michael Flynn & Bridget Reading)
Bridget, Jan. 1871 (civil record), Cloonalough, Kiltullagh Parish
Mary, July 1872 (civil record, Mary Gormley present)

Note: Michael was the son of James Gormley of Cloonalough in Kiltullagh Parish. Bridget was the daughter of John Waldron of Derrynacong.

William Hunt & Mary Hunt
m. Jan. 1872 (Patrick Gildea & Rose Daly)
Bridget, Augt. 1874 (Mark & Anne Hunt)
John, March 1876 (John & Kate Hunt)
Celia, March 1878 (Murty Hunt & Bridget Hunt)
Mary, March 1881 (Thomas Golden & Kate Hunt)
Thomas Michael, Sept. 1884 (Pat & Mary Fitzmaurice)

Note: William was the son of Thomas Hunt, dec'd., of Derrynacong. Mary was the daughter of Murty Hunt of Lecarrow. Celia Hunt of Lecarrow is present in many of the civil records of births.

John William Quinn & Bridget Grogan
m. Feb. 1873 (James Grogan & Mary Grogan)

John William was the son of William Quinn of Derrynacong. No civil record has been located for this marriage.

Peter Kedian & Mary Kearns (Kerins)
m. Feb. 1873 (John Hunt & Mary Grogan)
Catherine, Augt. 1874 (William Murphy & Ann Kearns)
Patrick, Oct. 1877 (Ned Connell &? Kearns)
Bridget, Dec. 1879 (James & Bridget Kearns; Patrick Kedian present)
Michael, Sept. 1882 (civil record; Mary Fitzmaurice present)
John Thomas, Oct. 1884 (Michael Tully & Margaret Kedian)

Note: Peter was the son of Patrick Kedian of Derrynacong. Mary was the daughter of Patrick Kearns of Derrynacong.

Austin Waldron & Kate Judge

m. Feb. 1875 (Michael Hopkins & Honor Judge)
Margaret, Dec. 1875 (Thomas & Honora Judge)

Note: Austin was the son of John Waldron of Derrynacong. Mary was the daughter of Murty Judge of Carrowreagh.

James Waldron & Catherine Fitmaurice
m. Feb. 1876 (Pat Tully & Kate Lyons)
Bridget, Apr. 1877 (Thomas O'Connell & Mary Dyer)
Mary, Augt. 1878 (Pat Dyer & Catherine Tully)
John, Feb. 1880 (Michael Kedian & Honora Waldron)
James, Sept. 1882 (Pat Fitzmaurice & Kate Bones; Mary Fitzmaurice present)
Catherine, Oct. 1884 (Pat Fitzmaurice & Mary Kelly)
Honoria, Oct. 1886 (John Fitzmaurice & Mary Hunt)
Patrick, June 1889 (Pat Fitzmaurice & Kate Lynskey)

Note: James was the son of James Waldron & Catherine Dyer of Brackloon. He was baptized in Augt. 1844 (David & Bartl. Hunt, sps.). A brother, Michael, was baptized in 1849 (Pat Forde & Bridget Freeman, sps.). Catherine was the daughter of Patrick Fitzmaurice & Mary Waldron of Derrynacong.

Michael Kearns (Kerins) & Ellen Connell
m. Feb. 1876 (James Kearns & Celia Kedian)
Honoria, Sept. 1880 (Peter Connell & Mary Kearns)
John, Oct. 1882 (Pat Kearns & Mary Waldron)
child, July 1887 (civil record)

Michael was the son of Patrick Kearns of Derrynacong. Ellen was the daughter of Peter Connell of Derrynacong.

Michael Murphy & Celia Kedian
m. Feb. 1877 (Thomas Tarpey & Mary Naughton)

Patrick Moore & Catherine Waldron
Mary & Honora, Augt. 1877 (W. O'Connell & Ellen Tully; Thomas Waldron & Ann Moore)
Patrick, Augt. 1877 (civil record)

Note: The parish register gives the mother's name as Mary Fitzmaurice. The civil record gives the mother's name as Waldron. In Patrick's death record (1877) the father's townland is given as Currane, the mother's as Derrynacong. No civil record of the marriage has been found. All three children appear in the civil record in August 1877. Only Mary and Honora are listed in the parish book. No marriage record has been located.

Michael Kedian & Margaret Kelly
m. Oct. 1877 (Pat Belia & Kate Tully)
Mary, Oct. 1878 (Pat Belia & Kate Hunt; Ellen Kelly, grandmother, present)
Ellen, Sept. 1883 (civil record; Ellen Kelly)

Note: Michael was the son of Michael Kedian of Derrynacong. Margaret was the daughter of John Kelly of Derrynacong.

Michael Kedian & Ellen Kearns
Mary Anne, Dec. 1877 (James O'Connell & Mary Kearns)

Note: this record exists in the Annagh Parish register. There is no civil record.

John William Quinn & Kate Kelly
m. Jan. 1878 (Bernard McDermott & Patrick Cregg)
Mary, Nov. 1878 (Patrick Fitzmaurice & Bridget Kelly)
Thomas, Dec. 1880 (Patrick & Mary Fitzmaurice)
Bridget, Apr. 1884 (Pat & Bridget Kelly)
Patrick, July 1887 (Pat Hunt & Catherine Waldron)
Kate, Oct. 1889 (John Waldron & Bridget Kelly)

Note: John William was the son of William Quinn of Derrynacong. Kate was the daughter of Patrick Kelly & Bridget Crane of Cloonalough, Kiltullagh Parish.

John Prenty & Ellen Hunt
m. May 1882 (John Waldron & Mary Rodgers)

Note: John was the son of Arthur Prenty & Bridget Waldron of Tooraree. He was born Augt. 1861. Ellen was the daughter of James & Honora Hunt of Derrynacong. She was born April 1858 (Thomas Fitzmaurice &Biddy

Morley). She died in May 1903. They resided in Toraree. John subsequently married Katherine Hunt, the daughter of Mark Hunt of Moneymore, in Augt. 1908. John died in Dec. 1944.

Thomas Curley & Bridget Fitzmaurice
John, July, 1884 (John & Honora Fitzmaurice; Mary Fitzmaurice present)

James Connell & Anne Kearns
m. Feb. 1884 (Patrick Fitzmaurice & Mary Waldron)
Edward, Dec. 1884 (Peter Kedian & Mary Tully)
Mary, Dec. 1886 (Peter Connell & Mary C?)
Kate, Dec. 1890 (Patrick & Kate Kedian)

Note: James was the son of Peter Connell of Derrynacong. Anne was the daughter of Patrick Kearns of Derrynacong.

Thomas Hunt & Mary Regan
m. Feb. 1884 (James Hunt & Julia Grogan)
John, Jan. 1885 (John Regan & Mary Anne Kenny)
Honoria, Dec. 1885 (? Hunt & Mary Regan)
Thomas, Augt. 1891 (Michael & Mary Regan)
Michael Francis, Sept. 1897 (Francis Regan & Mary Kelly; John Regan present)

Note: Thomas was the son of James Hunt of Derrynacong. Mary was the daughter of Patrick Regan of Killunagher.

Thomas Forde & Mary Hunt
m. May 1884 (Michael Tully & Kate Fitzmaurice)
Bridget, Jan. 1888 (Hugh Hunt & Maggie Tully)
Mary Ellen, July 1889 (James & Kate Waldron)
Patrick Austin, Augt. 1892 (Pat & Bridget Fitzmaurice)
Kate Agnes, Dec. 1893 (Michael Hunt & Mary Fitzmaurice)
Delia, (Kate's twin) Dec. 1893 (Pat Tully & Mary Waldron)
John, Jan. 1896 (John & Delia Waldron)

Note: Thomas was the son of Patrick Forde & Bridget Freeman of Derrynacong. Mary was the daughter of Pat Hunt & Bridget Fitzmaurice of Laughil, Kiltullagh Parish. Patrick married Catherine Griffin of Ballybunion in Hoboken, New Jersey, in Apr. 1913. Kate married John Flynn of Carrick in Augt. 1929.

John Deasy & Mary Cox
m. Dec. 1889 (Alfred Dyer? & Mary Dyer)
Thomas, Nov. 1890 (civil record; Kate Cox present)
Patrick, Apr. 1892 (Thomas Cox & Anne Deasy)
Bridget, May 1894 (Bridget & Delia Kedian; Mary Ford present)
Catherine, June 1896 (John Murphy & Bridget Cox)
John Austin, Sept. 1898 (Pat Tully & Mary Deasy; Kate Cox present)
Catherine, June 1900 (Pat Waldron & Kate Kedian)
Michael, 1903 [no civil record has been located]

Note: John was the son of Thomas Deasy, dec'd., of Cartron. Mary was the daughter of James Cox, dec'd., & Bridget Hunt of Derrynacong.

Peter Kedian & Bridget Clarke
Celia, Dec. 1890 (civil record)

Michael Regan & Mary Fitzmaurice
m. Jan. 1891 (Francis Regan & Mary Fitzmaurice)
Patrick, July 1892 (Pat Fitzmaurice & Mary Regan)
Mary Jane, Oct. 1894 (civil record)
Michael, Sept. 1897 (Pat Fitzmaurice & Mary Anne Finnegan)

Note: Michael was the son of Patrick Regan of Killunagher. Mary was the daughter of Pat Fitzmaurice of Derrynacong. Mary Jane married Thomas Joseph Ganley in the United States.

James Joseph Ganley & Ellen Kearns (nee Connell)
m. Oct. 1892 (Edward McGann & Kate Flynn)
Michael, Sept. 1893 (John & Delia Waldron)
Kate, May 1896 (John Kearns & Mary Boyle)
James, Oct. 1898 (Ned & Mary Connell)
Patrick, Oct. 1901 (John Grogan & Margaret Waldron)
Peter, Apr. 1904 (John & Bridget Boyle)

Note: James was the son of Patrick Ganley of Ballyhaunis. Ellen, a widow, was the daughter of Peter Connell of Derrynacong.

Peter Kedian & Elizabeth Prendergast
m. May 1894 (Hugh Hunt & Ellen Prendergast)

Note: Peter, a widower, was the son of Patrick Kedian of Derrynacong. Elizabeth was the daughter of Thomas Prendergast & Bridget Ferrick (Fannick?) of Greenwood. She was born Feb. 1864.

Thomas Ganley & Ellen Boland
m. Feb. 1895 (John Healey & Mary Boland)
Anne, Nov. 1896 (William Boland & Jane Ganley)
Kate, Sept. 1898 (John Fitzmaurice &? Boland)
Ellen, Dec. 1900 (Thomas Boland & Mary Dyer)
Jane & Bridget, Sept. 1903 (John Ruane & Mary Boland)

Note: Thomas was the son of John Ganley of [illegible], County Roscommon. He was described in the marriage record as a "railroad laborer." Ellen was the daughter of William Boland of Derrynacong.

Thomas Hunt & Anne Boland
m. March 1896 (William Forde & Kate Cox)
Patrick, Jan. 1897 (John Hunt & Mary Hunt)
John, Jan. 1898 (Thomas Hunt & Mary Hunt)
Kate, Dec. 1899 (Thomas Kilfoyle & Anne Caulfield)
Bridget, Augt. 1903 (William Boland & Mary Fitzmaurice)
Anne, Oct. 1906 (Patrick & Kate Maguire)

Note: Thomas was the son of John Hunt of Reask. Anne was the daughter of Patrick Boland & Bridget McGuire of Derrynacong.

Patrick Tully & Anne Griffin
m. March 1896 (Michael Fahy & Catherine Healy)
Catherine, Sept. 1897 (Edward Connell & Anne Tully)
Michael Patrick, Sept. 1898 (Patrick Dyer & Mary E. Dyer)
Bridget, May 1900 (Thomas Fahy & Bridget Fahy)
James, Oct. 1903 (Thomas Deasy & Celia Kedian)

William, Dec. 1907 (John Waldron & Delia Grogan)

Note: Patrick was the son of Patrick Tully of Brackloon. His mother was likely Bridget Green. Anne was the daughter of Matthew Griffin of Cloongonagh?

Thomas Forde & Bridget Lyons
m. Nov. 1897 (John Waldron & Anne Higgins)
Anne, Sept. 1898 (James Waldron & Catherine Bones)
Honoria, Jan. 1900 (Edward Lyons & Mary Higgins)
Rose, Dec. 1901 (Michael Lyons & Mary Ellen Forde)
Agnes, Dec. 1903 (Hubert Forde & Catherine Lyons)

Note: Thomas, a widower, was the son of Patrick Forde & Bridget Freeman of Derrynacong. He had been previously married to Mary Hunt. Bridget Lyons was the daughter of Edward Lyons and Catherine Bones of Larganboy. Anne married John McNamara in New York City in 1939. Honoria married John O'Boyle in New York City in 1931.

John Murphy & Ellen Fitzmaurice
m. Feb. 1898 (Michael Connor & Kate Fitzmaurice)
Catherine, Augt. 1905 (John Ryan & Kate Murphy)
Ellen, Nov.1906 (Michael McDonagh & Maggie Ryan)
Nora, Feb. 1908 (Patrick McDonagh & Mary J. Waldron)
Anne, 1912 (Patrick McDonagh & Mary McDonagh)

Note: John was the son of James Murphy of Killunagher. His age was given as 27. Ellen was the daughter of John Fitzmaurice of Derrynacong. Her age was given as 28. Anne married in Belmont, Mass. in 1940.

Michael Caulfield & Mary Waldron
m. Feb. 1899 [record needs verification]
Mary Anne, Nov. 1904 (Patrick Duffy & Anne Duffy)
James, Sept. 1907 (William Grealy? & Ellen Ganley)

Note: Mark Caulfield was the son of?? of County Roscommon. Mary Waldron was the daughter of James Waldron & Catherine Fitzmaurice of Derrynacong. No civil record of the marriage has been located. Mary Anne married John Regan in Ballyhaunis, year unknown.

Patrick Lyons & Bridget Hunt
m. Oct. 1900 (Martin Higgins & Mary Hunt)

Note: Patrick was the son of Patrick Lyons of Brackloon. Bridget was the daughter of William & Mary Hunt of Derrynacong.

Patrick Glavey & Kate Hunt
m. Feb. 1902 (John Waldron & Eleanor Florence Hunt)

Note: Patrick Glavey was the son of Thady Glavey of Aghamore. Kate Hunt was the daughter of William & Mary Hunt of Derrynacong.

John Fitzmaurice & Ellen Flatley
m. March 1902 (Martin Fitzmaurice & Catherine Walsh)
Mary Agnes, July 1903 (Thomas Flatley &? Fitzmaurice)
John, July 1905 (John Murphy & Bridget Flatley)
Bridget, Sept. 1906 (Martin Fitzmaurice & Ellen Waldron)
Ellen, Nov. 1908 (Martin Grogan & Daniel F -?)
Rose Anne, March 1910 (Patrick Regan & Mary Fitzmaurice)
Nora, Feb. 1912 (Thomas Ganley &? Ganley)
Margaret, Sept. 1913 (James Paisley & Joseph Paisley)

Note: John was the son of John Fitzmaurice & Mary Grealy of Derrynacong. Ellen was the daughter of William Flatley & Bridget Grogan of Lassiney. She was born March 1872. Mary may have married Thomas Hoban, year unknown.

Patrick Grogan & Delia Waldron
m. Jan. 1903 (Michael Grogan & Kate Waldron)
James Anthony, Nov. 1905 (John & Ellen Fitzmaurice)
Catherine, Oct. 1907 (Patrick Waldron & Nora Waldron)

Note: Patrick was the son of John Grogan & Bridget Cruise of Spaddagh. He was born Sept. 1873. Delia was the daughter of James Waldron & Catherine Fitzmaurice of Derrynacong. James married in Dublin in 1946. Catherine married in Dublin in 1935.

John Connally & Margaret Waldron
m. Feb. 1903 (Thomas Connally & Ellie Henekin)

Kate, Jan. 1906 (Thomas & Kate Connolly)
Mary Ellen, July 1907 (Patrick Flanagan & Nora Kedian)
Patrick, 1909 (Michael Connally & Ellen Connally)
John, Sept. 1912 (James Connally & Kate Connally)
Michael, Feb.1914 (Patrick Ganley & Kate Ganley)
Mary, June 1916 (civil record)

Note: John was the son of Michael Connally of Derrynacong. (His mother may be Bridget Boyle.) Margaret was the daughter of Austin Waldron of Killunagher. (Her mother may have been Mary Hunt.)

Nora Fitzmaurice & Thomas Flatley
m. June 1903 (Willie Flatley & Ellen Ryan)

Note: Nora was the daughter of John Fitzmaurice of Derrynacong. Thomas was the son of William Flatley of Lassiney. He was brother to Ellen Flatley who married Nora's brother, John. (See above.)

James Kenny & Mary Ellen Hunt
m. Feb. 1906 (Joseph Hunt & Rita Spelman)
James, Apr. 1907 (John Thomas Hunt & Nora Tighe)
Mary, June 1908 (Michael Tighe & Nora Tighe)

Note: James was the son of Patrick Kenny & Mary Frehily of Derrynacong. Mary Ellen was the daughter of Patrick Hunt, dec'd, of Lecarrow. Mary married Bernard Hunt in 1944.

James Kedian & Mary Tarpey
m. May 1913 (Michael Anthony Dyer & Maggie Tarpey)
Mable, May 1914 (James Tarpey & Delia Kedian)
Patrick, June, 1915 (Thomas Boland & M. Boland)
Daniel, Nov. 1916 (Daniel Tarpey & Bridget Kedian)
Michael, May 1920 (Edward Dyer & Delia Dyer)
Mary, July 1921 (Patrick Kearns & Ellen Kearns)

Note: James was the son of Patrick Kedian of Derrynacong. Mary was the daughter of Daniel Tarpey & Mary Lyons of Carrowkeel. She was born in August 1888.

Patrick Freeley & Anne Hunt
m. Nov. 1913 (John Thomas Freeley & Mary Dillon)
Jerome, June 1916 (Peter Freely & M. Kenny)
John, Sept. 1918 (Michael Tighe & Anne Tighe)
Patrick, March 1922 (Luke Tighe & Delia Tighe)

Note: Patrick was the son of John Freeley & Maggie Tarpey? of Derrynacong. Anne was the daughter of Patrick Hunt of Lecarrow.

James Ganley & Lizzie Kedian
m. Feb. 1920 (James Healy & Katie Quinn)

Note: James was the son of James Ganley of Derrynacong. Lizzie, a widow, was the daughter of Thomas Prendergast & Bridget Ferrick? of Greenwood.

Patrick Dyer & Bridget Henehan
m. Dec. 1921 (Dunmore, County Galway)
John Stephen, Dec. 1922
Mary Helena, July 1924
Delia Teresa, Augt. 1926
Margaret Christina, Dec. 1928
Katherine Josephine, March 1931

Note: No civil record of this marriage has been found. Patrick was the son of Patrick Dyer & Ellen Lyons of Brackloon South. He was born March 1884. He owned the first motorcar in Derrynacong and was a building contractor by profession. Information supplied by Margaret Conroy in *Brackloon a Trip Down Memory Lane* (2013, pp. 46-47).

John Flynn & Delia Kedian
m. Jan. 1923 (Joseph Cullen & Mary Jane Dyer)

Note: John was the son of Timothy Flynn & Margaret Lyons of Carrick, Kiltullagh Parish. He was born April 1870 and died in Feb. 1950. Delia Kedian was the daughter of Michael Kedian of Derrynacong. They resided in Carrick, County Roscommon.

Patrick Hanlon & Kate Kelly
m. Apr. 1926 (John Grennan & Delia Forde)

Note: Patrick was the son of Patrick Hanlon & Mary Greally of Carrick townland, Killutagh Parish. He was born July, 1880. Kate was the daughter of John William Quinn, dec'd., & Kate Kelly of Derrynacong.

Michael Hunt & Anna Ganley
m. June 1926 (Edmund Morley & Jennie Ganley)

Note: Michael was the son of Thomas Hunt of Derrynacong. Anna was the daughter of Thomas Ganley & Ellen Boland of Derrynacong.

John Flynn & Kate Forde
m. Augt. 1929 (John Walsh & Delia Forde)

Note: John, a widower, was the son of Timothy Flynn & Margaret Lyons of Carrick, Kiltullagh Parish. Kate was the daughter of Thomas Forde & Mary Hunt of Derrynacong. They resided in Carrick.

Edward Hanlon & Mary Deasy
m. Jan. 1931 (John Fitzmaurice & Anne Hanlon)

Note: Edward, age 31, was the son of Patrick Hanlon of Louth. Mary, age 29, was the daughter of John Deasy of Derrynacong.


Derrynacong Deaths – Civil records (informants are in parentheses)

William Quinn, Jan. 1868, 60, married (John Quinn, son)
Mary Connell, Feb. 1868, 40, (Peter Connell, husband)
Martin Waldron, first quarter 1869, 70, married (James Waldron)
Bridget (Grogan) Quinn, Sept. 1874, 25, married (John William Quinn, husband)
Patrick Moore, Jan. 1877, 29, married, (Currane, Catherine Waldron)
Michael Kedian, June 1877, 70, (Michael Kedian)
Thomas Freely (Frehily), Feb. 1881, 84, widower (Mary Kenny)
James Cox, Apr. 1882, 50, married (Mary Cox)
Honoria Hunt, Nov. 1882, 56, married (Thomas Hunt, son)
Patrick Boland, Oct. 1885, 22 (Bridget Boland, mother)
Patrick Boland, Dec. 1884, 65, married (Stephen Boland, son)
Patrick Kedian, Sept. 1885, 67, widower (Mary Kedian, daughter-in-law)
Mary Fitzmaurice, June 1886, 56 years, married (Mary Fitzmaurice, daughter)

Mary (Kearns) Kedian, March 1887, 33, married (Peter Kedian, husband)
Child Kearns, July 1887, 1 day (Ellen Kearns)
Bridget (Hunt) Cox, Jan. 1888, 60, widow (Mary Cox, daughter)
Child Connell, Oct. 1889, 1 day (Honor Kearns, grandmother)
Michael Kedian, Jan. 1892, 9, (Peter Kedian, father)
Bridget (Clarke) Kedian, Sept. 1893, 35, (Peter Kedian, husband)
James Waldron, March 1894, 53, married (Mary Waldron, daughter)
Patrick Kedian, Augt. 1895, 10, (Bridget Kedian, mother)
James Hunt, Feb. 1897, 70, widower (Mary Hunt, daughter-in-law)
Patrick Kearns, Apr. 1897, 70, married (Ellen Ganley, daughter-in-law)
Honor Kearns, Apr. 1897, 70, widow (Ellen Ganley, daughter-in-law)
John Waldron, Dec. 1897, 77, widower (Catherine Waldron)
Martin Dyer, Augt. 1900, 68, married (James Murphy)
Peter Connell, March 1903, 66, widower (Catherine Waldron, cousin)
Catherine Waldron, April 1903, 50, wife of Austin (Maggie Connolly, daughter)
Mary Fitzmaurice, Feb. 1904, 63, widow (Catherine Waldron, daughter)
John Joe Grogan, Feb. 1904, 3 months (Catherine Waldron, grandmother)
Margaret Waldron, Apr. 1905, 62, widow (Mary Caulfield, daughter)
John Fitzmaurice, July 1905, 68, married (John Fitzmaurice, son)
Patrick Fitzmaurice, Nov. 1906, 83, widower (Mary Regan, daughter)
William Boland, June 1908, 74, widower of Anne (Ellen Ganley, daughter)
Mary Kenny, Jan. 1907, 66, wife of Patrick (James Kenny, son)
Mary Fitzmaurice, Apr. 1917, 83, widow of John (Mary Fitzmaurice, daughter)
Mary Fitzmaurice, Jan. 1918, 40, single (Ellen Fitzmaurice, sister-in-law)
Austin Waldron, March 1918, 72, widower (Maggie Connolly, daughter)
Peter Kedian, Nov. 1918, 72, (Lizzie Kedian, wife)
Bridget Boland, Apr. 1918, 70, widow of Patrick (Annie Hunt, daughter)
Patrick Kedian, Feb. 1920, 72, (Bridget Kedian, wife)
Ellen Ganley, Sept. 1924, 70, married (Katie Caulfield, daughter)
John William Quinn, Jan. 1925, 75, married, (Kate Quinn, daughter)
Bridget Kedian, March 1927, 78, widow (Mary Kedian, daughter-in-law)
Katherine Quinn, Dec. 1927, 78, widow, (Kate Hanlon, daughter)
Delia (Kedian) Flynn, July 1928, 40, (John Flynn, husband, Carrick)
John Connolly, Augt. 1934, 62, married, (Mary Connolly, daughter)
Mary Hunt, March 1935, 74, married (Michael Hunt, son)
John Deasy, Jan. 1937, 73, married (Mary Hanlon, daughter)
Mary Deasy, Augt. 1938, 78, widow (Swinford Hospital)
Thomas Forde, May 1939, 82, widow (Delia Forde, daughter)

Patrick Tully, Jan. 1939, 70, (Anne Tully, wife, in Devlis)
Michael Hunt, Sept. 1939, 52, married, son of Thomas Hunt & Mary Regan (Dublin)
James Ganley, Augt. 1943, 79, widower (Nora Kearns, step-daughter)
Michael Caulfield, Augt. 1943, 80, married, (James Caulfield, son)
Ellen Kenny, June 1945, 68, married (James Kenny, husband)
Anne Tully, Apr. 1948, 82, widow of Patrick, (Michael Tully, son)
Thomas Patrick Hoban, Apr. 1951, infant, (Thomas Hoban, father)
Mary Caulfield, Feb. 1955, 86, widow, (Ann Caulfield, daughter)
Ellen Fitzmaurice, Dec. 1956, 85, widow, (Thomas Hoban, son-in-law)
Margaret Conolly, Jan. 1958, 83, widow (Michael Conolly, son)
James Kenny, May 1958, 88, widower, (Bryan Hunt, son-in-law)
Anne (Boland) Hunt, May 1959, 84, widow (John Hunt, son)


Friary Cemetery

James Waldron, Apr. 1925 [no civil record found]
Catherine Waldron, Feb. 1917, 67, (Delia Grogan, daughter)
James Waldron Jr., May 1968

Bridget Hunt, Nov. 1855, 66, wife of Thomas Hunt
William Hunt, Nov. 1914, 84, (Thomas Michael Hunt, son)
Mary Hunt, Nov. 1931, wife of William Hunt [no civil record found]
John William Hunt, June 1923 [no civil record found]
Thomas M. Hunt, Nov. 1918 [no civil record found]

Note: stone originally erected by Michael Hunt, son of Thomas & Bridget Hunt. Thomas Hunt may have died in 1867. Another notation has stone erected by their daughter Mrs. K. Glavey of Aghamore.


New Cemetery

Patrick Hunt, Jan. 1924 [no civil record found]
Baby Tommie Hunt, Oct. 1939 [no civil record found]
Anne (Boland) Hunt, March 1959, 82, widow (John Hunt, son)
John Hunt, March 1983

Ellen Ganley, Apr. 1936, 76, married (Jennie Ganley, daughter)
Thomas Ganley, 1951 [no civil record found]
Jane Fitzmaurice, 1977
John Fitzmaurice, 1989

Patrick Hanlon, Feb. 1959, 79, (Kathleen Fitzmarris)
Catherine Hanlon, Feb. 1974, 86
Joseph Hanlon, Oct. 1947, 19, (Patrick Hanlon)
William Fitzharris, 1991, 64
Kathleen Fitzharris, March 1998, 68

John Freeley, 1923, 6, (Annie Freeley, mother)
Patrick Freeley, Dec. 1944, 62, (Jerome Freeley, son)
Annie Freeley, Apr. 1951, 63, (Patrick Freeley, son)
Jerome Freeley, July 1955, 39, (Clagnagh, Sarah Freeley, wife)

Michael Regan, Sept. 1926, 30, (Patrick Regan, brother)
Mary Regan, Dec. 1942, 83, 1942, married (Patrick Regan, son)
Michael Regan, Apr. 1947, 84, widower (Patrick Regan, son)

Note: Michael died in an accident involving falling sand.

Infant Dyer, 1930 [no civil record found]
Patrick Dyer, Feb. 1961, 76, married (John Dyer, son)
John Stephen Dyer, August 2002
Delia Dyer, 2004
Mary Helena Brown, March 1995
Delia Teresa Conroy, Sept. 1999
Katherine Josephine McIntyre, Dec. 1988


Forde deaths

Bridget Forde, March 1889, 1
Mary (Hunt) Forde, Apr. 1897, 43
John Forde, Augt. 1897, 1
Bridget (Lyons) Forde, March 1920, 54
Thomas Forde, May 1939, 82 (New Cemetery)

Nora (Forde) O'Boyle, Sept. 1973, 73, New York
Rose Forde, Feb. 1974, 73 Bronx, NY
Agnes Forde, July 1977, 73, Bronx NY
Patrick Forde, Jan. 1980, 87, Hoboken, NJ
Kate (Forde) Flynn, June 1981, 87, (New Cemetery)
Delia Forde, Oct. 1981, 87, (New Cemetery)


Search for Missing Friends Column (Boston newspaper):

Nov. 1852 – of Thomas Hunt, native of Derrynacull, near Ballyhavnis (Co. Mayo) who came to America in 1847 – he lived 2 years at Reading, PA – supposed now to be in Lancaster County, PA. Any information of him will thankfully be recieved by his brother Patrick Hunt, Roxbury, Massachusetts.


Petty Court Records

[By permission of: Transcripts (c) IIMI & FMP, Images (c) NAI, available on Findmypast]

Note: complainants are listed first, defendants second. Unless other specified, all individuals were from Derrynacong. The date indicated may refer to the court date or to the date of theinfraction.

Thomas John Quick, Esq. vs. Mark Dyer. Defendant kept a kiln for "drying of corn" at Brackloon without proper license. Deferred fine or three months imprisonment. 25 Jan. 1856.

Martin Bride of Culnacleha vs. Michael Bride of Culnacleha and Michael Fitzmaurice. Violent assaut at Culnacleha. 12 Jan. 1858.

James Hunt vs. William Boland. Defendant owed wages for two days ploughing. 2 Sept. 1861.

Michael Fitzmaurice vs. John McGarry of Cooloher?. Assault at Ballyhaunis. 20 Jan. 1863.

James Boland vs. William Boland. Defendant took chest containing oats. 1 March 1864.

Pat Hunt of Brackloon vs. Michael Kedian, Michael Dyer & Mary Kedian. "Violent threats & abusive language which put complainant in terror of his life." 5 June 1864.

Constable Charles Goldrick vs. William Boland. Dedendant intoxicated at Pollnacroaghy. 11 Dec. 1869.

John Waldron vs. Michael Grogan of Killunaugher. Complainant owed 1 pound 19 shillings for a pig sold. 2 May 1870.

Stephen Healy and James Grennan of Arlour? vs. William Boland of Crossbeg. Assault at Kilmannin. 14 May 1870.

John Sloyan vs. John Kelly. Defendant owed 0-19-3 for "shop goods and cash" in the years 1871 & 1872. 14 May 1872.

John Drudy of Lurgan vs. Hugh Cox and Patrick Kelly. Defendants did "unlawfully assault and rob the complainant of a two shilling piece." 12 Oct. 1873.

John Drudy vs. Hugh Forde. The defendant did "aid and abet Hugh Cox and Patrick Kelly" in the assault and robbery of the two shilling pieces. 12 Oct. 1873.

Edward Wynne, Esq. vs. John Waldron. Intoxicated on the public street. 17 March 1874.

Bernard Flanagan of Ballyhaunis vs. James Hunt and Patrick Kedian. Possession of unlicensed dogs. 11 Apr. 1874.

Thomas Freely vs. Pat Fitzmaurice, Mary Fitzmaurice, Mary Fitzmaurice, Jr., and James Cox. Assault. May 1874.

Michael Kedian found intoxicated on a public street. 6 Dec. 1874.

Patrick Kearns found intoxicated on a public street. 21 Nov. 1876.

Peter Connell found intoxicated on a public street. 25 Jan., 1877.

Martin Dyer found intoxicated on a public street. 24 Apr. 1877.

John Fitzmaurice vs. James Cox. Defendant unlawfully permitted 55 hens to trepass on his crop of oats. Oct. 1877.

Thomas Ganley of Lisbane vs. John Quinn. Defendant owes sum of 0-7-7. 13 Jan. 1880.

Michael Waldron of Devlis, agent for the Guardians of the Poor, vs. John Deasy. Defendant neglected to pay sum of 2 -9-8 for seed rate. 5 Feb. 1890.

Viscount Dillon of Loughglynn vs. Michael Kedian. "You, the defendant did refuse and omit to quit and deliver up to complainant the owner thereof of all that??? lands of Derrynacong in the petty sessions district of Ballyhaunis, County of Mayo, into possession of which you had been put as caretaker by said complainant, his known agent or receiver, possession thereof having been demanded by complainant, his agent or receiver." A note reads in part: "Warrant to use ... directed by the High Sherrif of the County of Mayo for the eviction to be executed in a day not less than ..." June 1890.

The Queen vs. Stephen Boland. Defendant found intoxicated in the home of Ellen Kearns of Killunaugher. Ellen was charged with selling whiskey illegally. 5 Oct. 1890

Malachi Kelly found intoxicated on a public street. 16 Dec. 1890.

The Queen vs. Mary Waldron, Catherine Kedian, and Patrick Drury & Catherine Drury of Killunaugher. They were found on the premises of Ellen Kearns, who was illegally dealing in intoxicating liquor. 29 Jan. 1891.

Ellen Kearns was fined 1 pound, seven shillings, for selling intoxicating liquor, "to wit, spirits and porter," without a license. 29 Jan. 1891.

Peter Fitzmaurice, born in Derrynacong in 1827, sentenced to three months for stealing bog bran. He resided in Cherryfield. 5'7 in height, 163 lbs., brown-gray hair, hazel eyes. Augt. 1891.

Sgt. Edward Sweeney, officer weights & measures, vs. Ellen Kearns. Defendant had weights and scales in her shop that were not verified. 2 June 1892.

Michael Wadron of Devlis vs. Thomas Forde. Defendant neglected to pay the sum of twelve shillings for the seed rate. October 1892.

William Boland vs. James Ganley. Defendant owes plaintiff sum of 1-0-0 for cash lent and for meat sold in Dec. 1892. 6 Feb. 1893.

Michael Waldron vs. James Waldron. Defendant neglected to pay sum of 6 shillings for seed rate. 11 July 1893.

John Quinn vs. Patrick Leonard of Gurteenmore. Assault. 27 Sept. 1893.

James Kenny of Cappagh vs. Patrick Kenny. Assault at Ballyhaunis. 19 March 1895.

Anne Connell vs. Peter Connell. Assault. 25 April 1895. (On same day, Peter Connell counter-charged Anne Connell with assault.)

Anne Connell vs. Ellen Ganley. Assault. 6 May 1895. (Ellen Ganley counter-charged Anne on the same day.)

Michael Waldron of Devlis vs. John Quinn. Defendant has neglected to pay sum of 14 shillings for seed rate. 21 Jan. 1896.

Patrick Finnegan of Lurgan vs. William Boland. Defendant allowed horse to trepass on complainant's crop of potatoes and oats. 19 May 1896.

John Fitzmaurice vs. John Deasy. Defendant allowed two asses to prepass on complainant's property. 23 July 1896.

Patrick Finnegan of Lurgan vs. Thomas Ganley. The use of threatening language, putting the complainant in bodily fear. 26 Augt. 1897. (Thomas Ganley counter-charged with same complaint.)

Patrick Finnegan of Lurgan vs. William Boland. Assault at Ballyhaunis. 13 Sept. 1897

William Hunt found intoxicated on a public street in Ballyhaunis. 9 Nov. 1897. (Sgt. Patrick Lyons)

Martin Fitzmaurice found intoxicated in the licensed premises of James Greally of Ballyhaunis. 25 Jan. 1898 (Sgt. Patrick Lyon).

Michael Waldron of Devlis vs. James Ganley (reps. of Patrick Kearns). Defendant failed to pay 1 pound 4 shillings. 27 Feb. 1898.

John Cribbin of Moneymore vs. Patrick Tully. Assault at Moneymore. 7 July 1898.

James Ganley neglected to pay 1 pound 4 shillings for seed rate on 2 Nov. 1898.

William Boland vs. Patrick Finnegan of Lurgan. Allowed three pigs to walk on complainant's property. 5 May 1899.

Anne Tully vs. John Cribbin Sr., John Cribben Jr. & Luke Cribbin, all of Moneymore. Assault and threatening language. 16 June 1899.

Patrick Kedian vs. John Waldron. Defendant used threatening and abusive language. The defendant should "show cause why he should not be bound to keep the peace and be of good behavior." 14 Nov. 1899.

Patrick Kedian vs. Thomas Hunt. Assault at Ballyhaunis. 17 March 1901.

John Kenny of Gurtenbeg vs. James Ganley. Assault at Ballyhaunis. 25 Sept. 1906.

Thomas Ganley vs. Patrick Moran of Killunaugher and John Drudy of Lurgan. Assault at Spaddagh. 28 Augt. 1907.

John Drudy of Lurgan vs. William Boland. Allowed five head of cattle to trepass on complainant's land. 3 Jan. 1908.

Thomas Hunt neglected to pay 1-5-6 for seed rate. 20 Jan. 1908.

County Council at Castlebar vs. John Waldron, James Waldron & Patrick Lyons of Spaddagh. Defendants neglected to repair "240 perches of road from Loughglynn Road at Brackloon East to Waldron's house at Derrylahan." 3 Feb. 1908.

John Murphy vs. Anne Hunt. Assault. 10 June 1908. (On same day, Anne Hunt counter-charged John Murphy & Ellen Murphy for assault.)

John Deasy vs. Thomas Flanagan of Ballyhaunis. Defendant owed five shillings for "the cutting and spreading of turf" in June 1909.

Ellen Ganley was found intoxicated at Ballyhaunis. 30 Jan. 1912. Fined five shillings.

John Quinn vs. Thomas Forde. Defendant allowed three head of cattle to trepass on "land cropped with oats," causing damage in the amount 4 shillings. 26 Augt. 1912.


Undated Sligo Prison Record

James Ganley and Peter Ganley were imprisoned for four months with the charge of robbing John Jordan. Both were born and raised in Derrynacong. James was described as 25, 5'7, 140 lbs. with dark hair, blue eyes and a fresh complexion. He was married to "Lizzie." Peter was described as 22, 5'8, 143 lbs. with dark hair, brown eyes and a fresh complexion. His wife was "Mary."


From the Brackloon School Manuscript. (1937, 1938)

Teresa Dyer wrote:

"I live in the village of Derrynacong in the parish of Ballyhaunis, in the barony of Costello and in the County of Mayo. There are eighteen houses in the village of Derrynacong. Seven are slated and the others thatched. There is one lake in the village, in Patrick Freeley's land, which was once owned by James Murphy. There is a story about that lake. There was once a rich man who had a castle where the lake now stands and he was very unkind to the poor. One day a magician came to his house dressed like a beggar and begged for bread which the rich man refused. So the magician changed him into a swan and his house into a lake."

Teresa Dyer wrote:

"There is a pathway that leads from our house in Drrynacong to Cribben's in Moneymore. It is said that numerous armies passed along that pathway in search of the people who attended Mass in Ballyhaunis Friary. There is another road which leads from Grogan's in Derrynacong to Cribben's in Moneymore. It is also believed that there is a road which leads from a by-road to Forde's bog. It was a hiding place for the priests in penal days."

Regarding John Deasy:

One of the entries in the Brackloon School Manuscript collection concerns John Deasy. Information was provided by Thomas Forde (written by Francie Hoban of Lisbane):

"John Deacy was born in the year 1861 in the village of Coogue near Aghamore. When he was six years of age he went to school for about three months and then his father began to teach him to weave. He went to England when he was fourteen years old and he there joined the army, enlisting in 'The Connaught Rangers.' From England he went to India and spent seven years there. He traveled India, Japan, Africa, Spain, America and England, then he came home to Coogue and he married a girl called Mary Cox and went to live in her home in Derrynacong. Later he went to Castlebar and taught young soldiers to use the Martin Henry rifle, for which he got fifteen shillings a week. As he had only a few acres of land he took up his old trade, weaving. He made tweed, frieze, and blankets and sold them at the local markets. Practically every house in this district has some of his materials. Michael Regan is still wearing an overcoat made from his frieze cloth and his daughter's father-in-law never wore any other sort of coat. John stopped weaving six years ago when he got the pension. Weaving was the traditional trade of his family. He loved his native language and was never happier than when he had a crowd listening to his most interesting stories. He was a great singer and knew all the old Irish songs."

In a 1903 contest John won first prize in a local contest for a flannel he weaved.

<u>Parliamentary Papers House of Commons, Vol. 63, 1889</u>:

Patrick Fitzmaurice petitioned for a reduction in rent – from 3-2-0 to 2-0-0.
John Fitzmaurice petitioned for a reduction in rent – from 5-14-0 to 4-10-0.
Bridget Forde petitioned in reduction of rent – from 4-5-0 to 3-0-0.

<u>Additional Records</u>

*Annagh Parish* magazine reported that three nineteenth century teachers were from Derrynacong: James Groarke, Sr.; James Groarke, Jr., and Michael Connell. No civil records have been found for the Groarkes. A civil death record exists for Michael Connell in April 1883, townland of Lisbane. His profession was listed as teacher.

There is a June 1856 record in the Annagh Parish book for the baptism of Eleanor Kedian, daughter of Patrick Kedian & Kate Fitzmaurice. Name of townland not given

*Brackloon A Trip Down Memory Lane* (published 2013) describes family history and lore of the townlands in the vicinity of Derrynacong and it lists school children by townland from 1872 – 1912.